THE TEACHING MIRROR

LESSONS LEARNED AS A FIRST-YEAR TEACHER

Victor Z. Stanhope

Robert D. Reed Publishers . Bandon, OR

Copyright © 2019 by Victor Z. Stanhope

All Rights Reserved.

No part of this book may be reproduced without written permission from the publisher or copyright holders, except for a reviewer who may quote brief passages in a review; nor may any part of this book be reproduced, stored in a retrieval system, or transmitted in any form or by any means electronic, mechanical, photocopying, recording or other, without written permission from the publisher or copyright holders.

Robert D. Reed Publishers
P.O. Box 1992
Bandon, OR 97411
Phone: 541-347-9882; Fax: -9883
E-mail: 4bobreed@msn.com
Website: www.rdrpublishers.com

Editor/Formatter: Cleone Reed
Cover Designer: fiverr.com/lauria

Soft Cover: 978-1-944297-50-3

EBook: 978-1-944297-51-0

Library of Congress Control Number: 2019903033

Designed, Formatted, and Printed in the United States of America

DEDICATION

I dedicate this book to my students.
To the students who inspired me,
the students who challenged me,
and the students who humbled me.
You have all taught me invaluable things
and pushed me to become
an even better teacher and person.
I am grateful to have had
the opportunity to be your teacher.

ACKNOWLEDGMENTS

I would like to thank all of those who supported me with the writing, editing, and publication of this work. I would especially like to thank my colleagues for making this book possible, my dear friends and parents who helped in revising this work, and other loved ones for their consistent support. I am grateful for all of you.

TABLE OF CONTENTS

DEDICATION 3
ACKNOWLEDGMENTS 5
PREFACE 9
INTRODUCTION 11
LESSON 1 – DON'T LET TEACHING CONSUME YOUR LIFE. 17
LESSON 2 – SAY "YES" TO EVERYTHING. 23
LESSON 3 – BE FEARED AND BE LOVED. 31
LESSON 4 – BRING POSITIVITY, ENTHUSIASM, ENERGY, AND MORALE. 39
LESSON 5 – REGULARLY EXPERIENCE GOOD TEACHERS. .47
LESSON 6 – EMBRACE TECHNOLOGY. 53
LESSON 7 – ACCEPT STUDENTS AS *YOUR* RESPONSIBILITY. 63
LESSON 8 – MASTER TEACHING, NOT CONTENT. 71
LESSON 9 – REMAIN PRIVATE. 77
LESSON 10 – BE SELF-AWARE. 83
LESSON 11 – ANTICIPATE THE UNEXPECTED. 91

LESSON 12 – SET CLEAR EXPECTATIONS. 101

LESSON 13 – MAINTAIN YOUR CONFIDENCE. 113

LESSON 14 – MONITOR YOUR EMOTIONS. 121

LESSON 15 – PRIORITIZE EVALUATIONS. 129

LESSON 16 – MAKE IT RELEVANT. 141

LESSON 17 – FIND A FITTING ORGANIZATIONAL METHOD. 147

LESSON 18 – FIND A FITTING CLASSROOM MANAGEMENT STYLE. 153

LESSON 19 – EXPERIMENT. 161

LESSON 20 – BE REFLECTIVE. 167

FINAL THOUGHTS 173

ABOUT THE AUTHOR 175

PREFACE

"I am writing this paragraph of the preface exactly one week before starting my first day as a first-year teacher – and I am panicking. I went through years of college, read a few books over the summer regarding tips for the first year teaching, and asked former teachers what to expect. None yielded meaningful or de-stressing results. I think this book will serve to empathetically reflect on my emotions, fears, concerns, solutions, successes, and failures as a means to serve future first-year teachers. I can honestly say that I have no accurate prediction as to what this book will result in; I simply hope the finalized product is useful to others.

For the sake of brevity, I will simply outline my situation and why I think a book written about my experiences will be useful to others. I graduated summa cum laude in December of 2016 from my local state college with a bachelor's degree in history, a minor in psychology, and a K–12 Social Studies teaching certificate. In May, a high-ranking and prominent high school in America's northeast offered me a job. News outlets have ranked this high school as one of the top 50 high schools in the nation.

I, as a first-year teacher at this school, will be taking you through my journey so that you may be better prepared for your first year. Hopefully, if I even finish this book, you can find value in my experience and use lessons I have learned through my first year."

***

I am writing this paragraph almost one month *after* my first year teaching – and what an experience it was. As stated previously, the idea of this book was conceived from the absence of useful and meaningful resources for new first-year teachers. Over the summer, before the start of my first year teaching, I wasted too much time reading books that were void of practical, interesting, or sensible advice for first-year teachers. Though the resources included sound information for first-year teachers, there were absolutely no authentic examples provided to ground the information. For instance, when a book says, "Set high expectations for students," it seems like great advice – and it is. However, if the book does not go into *specific* examples as to how to achieve this, the advice is useless. I hope that this book provides first-year teachers with both sound advice and sound examples. Now that this book is complete, I can proudly and assuredly say that I believe my experiences, successes, and failures are extremely valuable to incoming first-year teachers.

INTRODUCTION

Anxious? I was too. The first year teaching feels like an insurmountable obstacle. The overwhelming "I have no idea what the hell I'm doing" feeling is incredibly disconcerting. As a recent first-year teacher currently heading into my second year, I can empathize with all of those emotions. While I cannot promise this book will completely quell those feelings, I can assure you that it will help.

This book stemmed from my own worries and lack of genuinely helpful resources. This book's aim is to do the following:

- provide incoming first-year teachers with an honest and practical perspective of the experience,
- connect with and address first-year teachers' emotions and worries,
- offer applied tips and exemplify their effectiveness, and
- illustrate my failures, remedies, successes, and learned lessons.

This book is an introspective and honest analysis of my first year's experiences synthesized into lessons learned from the endeavor – lessons that new first-year teachers, and others, can absorb and apply. The title, *The Teaching Mirror*, is as such because this book is a reflective piece that seeks to provide an understanding of life as a first-year teacher, and the emerging lessons from the experience. The rationale for including and analyzing both successes and failures is that both are essential for new teachers to encapsulate the experience of what it means to be a first-year teacher. Often, the failures yield more meaning than the successes. Some aspects of the book might seem memoir-esque, which I suppose it is in many ways. However, the instances in which I expand on personal examples serve to illuminate concrete instances for new teachers. Furthermore, this book is meant to be concise to allow first-year teachers to either read it during the summer prior to their start or throughout their first year teaching. A long, fluffed book is not what a first-year teacher wants or needs.

While the above describes what the book is, I think it is equally valuable to describe what this book is *not*. This is not an education textbook, or a book filled with educational theory – quite the opposite in many ways. Though I provide instructional advice throughout, this book serves more as a complement to educational theory books; it bridges gaps between theory and application. Furthermore, this book is not merely a chronology of my experiences during my first year teaching. It is, I hope, much more interesting and didactic.

I hope you find that this book is succinctly and comprehensively designed. Each chapter starts with the lesson learned from my experience, along with journal entries that relate to the lesson (more on the journal entries shortly). I will briefly introduce each lesson, and then delve into my failures and successes regarding the lesson. Lastly, I will close each chapter with a conclusion that provides a summary of the recommended strategies and my advice for first-year teachers.

In preparation for this book, I logged journal entries that outlined my thoughts, feelings, happenings, achievements, and blunders before and throughout my first year teaching. While the idea was originally to journal my experiences every day, it became more or less once a week due to a lack of time and/or energy – being a first-year teacher is a hard life. I must warn the reader that the entries are raw – with only personal information redacted – and can be somewhat dramatic. The first year is somewhat of an emotional wave, but I believe my thoughts at the time are valuable for new incoming teachers.

One needs some background knowledge to contextualize my experience. I was hired as a social studies teacher at a high-ranking high school in America's northeast. During my first year teaching, I was assigned typical general education classes, in which I taught alone, and collaborative classes, in which I acted as the collaborative teacher alongside a general education teacher. I taught Honors United States History I, Honors United States History II, and Honors Global Studies. My close colleague, Aaron, was the general education teacher in Honors Global Studies, and the teacher with whom I shared my classroom – he is mentioned and referenced throughout this book. Prior to his job at my current school district, Aaron served numerous years as a teacher and department chair at another school district. Aaron was an outstanding teacher, and I learned a lot from him. As such, my observations of Aaron guide many of my learned lessons, and I use these observations as examples for my lessons throughout the book.

I want to make it clear that my perspective on the first year teaching may be different from others. While I believe my experiences and included lessons will be of value to any new teacher, my school is undoubtedly unique. As one of the top high schools in the country, students were generally high achieving and relatively enthusiastic learners. I experienced much of the same stressors and worries as common first-year teachers, but I recognize that other districts, particularly low-income urban school areas, have a large set of additional or different concerns that are absent from my experience and this book.

So, how can you use this book? Why even bother going to the next page? You may look at the lessons on the Table of Contents page and feel as though they are obvious; "Of course I should be doing these things," you might think; "it just seems too easy." I thought the same way before my first year teaching. However, what do the lessons presented actually look like in practice? What does being reflective or being self-aware actually consist of? What are examples of a new teacher being reflective or self-aware? Or, better yet, what are some particular examples of a teacher failing at being reflective or self-aware? Furthermore, how does a first-year teacher feel throughout the year? What are some emotional stressors to be aware of during the first year teaching? That is where this book originates. Use this book to see my examples and experiences, and learn from the mistakes and achievements.

Lastly, I must mention that this book completely exposes me – and I am keenly aware of that. Every odd thought, negative emotion, and failure throughout my first year teaching is included in this book. While it is, at many points, embarrassing and uncomfortable for me to unveil these inadequacies, I know that doing so will better serve new first-year teachers. I will be the martyr, and hope that it serves future first-year teachers well.

LESSON 1 – DON'T LET TEACHING CONSUME YOUR LIFE.

Journal on November 4: "So, I haven't been writing because I have been so busy. Work, while many times super stressful and typically over 15 hours or so a day, has been okay..."

Journal on November 25: "I'm tired. This teaching thing along with trying to go to graduate school and juggling my personal life is taking a toll. I've been sick for the past week, and nearly called out today but decided against it. Every time I see my friends, my parents, or (my significant other), I am disappointed in myself; they have all been so great and supportive of me recently, and I don't have the time or energy to show my deep appreciation. I love aspects of teaching. I hate aspects of teaching. There's no doubt that, right now, it is slowly killing me..."

Introduction

When starting your first teaching job, there will be a seemingly impossible amount of work to do. From planning your next day's lesson, to planning the next unit, to grading – there is never enough time. To make sure it all is done, and done well, you may be compelled to go in early, stay late, and let the profession consume your life. Please do not let it; for the sake of your sanity, do not let it. The first year takes commitment and dedication, but it too often engulfs first-year teachers' lives. I will first discuss my workaholic schedule that I operated in for the first four months of my first year and its effects on my personal and professional life. Then, I will address how I overcame the long hours and recaptured my life during the second half of the year.

Failures

As illustrated in my journal entry in the introduction to this lesson, I often worked fifteen-hour days. From late September through November, I got to work at 7:15 a.m. and left around 6:00 p.m. I then commuted home and continued to work at least three or four hours at night. On top of my typical first year workload, I had graduate schoolwork, as my district requested that I obtain my special education certificate. The worst part about working these grueling hours is that, in hindsight, most of them were wasted. I unrealistically tried to change all the existing units in the curriculum and create original ones, including all the lessons, assessments, activities, and materials. It was a fruitless venture, and one I regret wholly. Those long hours severely affected my life personally and professionally.

In the personal arena, the long hours negatively affected my relationships, my hobbies, and my mindset. As described more personally in my journal entry, my relationships became disturbed. While I will not bore you with details, the time invested in my job put a distance between my partner and me. My bond with my family and friends also dwindled, as I had no time to allocate for preserving those relationships. Furthermore, the long hours stopped me from pursuing my hobbies. I had actively trained jiu-jitsu, played guitar, read, and played hockey – all of which stopped during the first few months of teaching. Because both my relationships and hobbies were in decline, my mindset shifted, which negatively affected my personal health. I found myself succumbing to temptations such as eating unhealthy foods, not sleeping for an adequate time, and spending more money while rationalizing these behaviors with the attitude of "I worked so hard today, and things have been so hard lately: I deserve it." These happenings, especially in the dark and gloomy months of the fall and winter in the northeast, temporarily caused emotional chaos. The eventual result was a slight mental breakdown (see Lesson 14).

The long working hours, counterintuitively, negatively affected me in the professional realm as well. Because I was trying to change all the units in my classes, I tried to balance planning the short term, such as the next day's lesson, with the long term, like the entire next unit. The result was that I was doing both poorly. My daily lesson plans started lacking substance as I tried allotting more time to planning future units. Furthermore, I was always incredibly tired at work due to exhaustion and the bad sleeping routine as described above. I could not concentrate effectively in class, and I felt as if I could not give students my full attention. Students commented a few times on my tired gaze and/or bags under my eyes. The long hours had not helped me prepare, feel confident, or succeed professionally. Rather, the hours were detrimental to my health, relationships, and career.

Successes

However, there does exist a happy balance between working hard and having a fulfilling personal life as a first-year teacher. Luckily, I found that happy medium during the second half of my first year – be it through desperation or revelation, I am still not sure. From the months of January through June, I never got to work before 7:30 a.m., and I never left after 5 p.m. I heavily limited the amount of work done at home; if it needed to be done, I tried to get it done at school. This might not be feasible during the first few weeks of your first year, but you should strive to reach this point by the middle of October. A big takeaway for me was to either go in early, or stay late – not both. You may choose to do either, but I would recommend staying late over arriving early – I think administrators notice more.

Through my new working schedule, my attitude shifted. Mornings before work were no longer dreadful, work was no longer painstaking, and I was a more engaging and effective teacher in the classroom. Even the most passionate of teachers will feel burned-out if they grossly overwork. Furthermore, my relationships grew, I partook in my favorite hobbies again, and my personal health improved. Please note that I did not stop planning units or discontinue my pursuit of instructional improvements on this new schedule. Rather, I was more aware of what I could and could not feasibly do, and used my time much more efficiently and systematically. I planned the week's lessons first, and then I would outline the next unit with whatever remaining time I had. Eventually, I could detail the next unit thoroughly, and it allowed me the time to pursue other activities that I enjoyed.

Conclusion

If you are an ambitious person, a perfectionist, or someone who takes pride in their work (as teachers typically are), you will be tempted to work very long hours during your first year. I assure you that choosing to work such long hours will negatively affect your personal and professional life. To streamline your work, set some rules that you are comfortable with for yourself. It might seem trivial and tedious, but setting concrete rules is the only way to create solid barriers to prevent professional encroachment into your personal life. Perhaps it is that you will only work at home twice per week, or that you will only grade a certain number of essays per night. I will include some rules that I set for myself below. Whatever those rules are, make clear boundaries for yourself *before* your first year. You can always adjust them during the first year, but if they are not set before your first year, they are much more difficult to follow. Nonetheless, if you do not set and adhere to rules, the profession will begin to consume your life; and it can lead to misery, severed relationships, and professional inadequacy. I will include a brief list of my own rules below.

My Rules

- Never get to work before 7:30 a.m.
- Always leave work before 5:00 p.m.
- Only work at home on Sundays and two weekdays.
- Relationships always come before work.
- Grade only 15 essays/assignments at a time.
- Search for resources for a maximum of 20 minutes per lesson.

LESSON 2 – SAY "YES" TO EVERYTHING.

Journal on August 31: "I am not sure if it is a good thing or a bad thing, but I have been asked to be involved in many additional activities at the school, and I haven't even started yet. For example, I have been asked to be an assistant class advisor for the junior class, a volunteer for a project to foster positive culture in the school, and to work after school on bus duty. The very first piece of advice I got from another teacher was, 'Be a good soldier. Do everything they want you to do when you are young and able to do it. Make yourself valuable to the school.' I said 'yes' to every opportunity that came my way. I am not sure if loading first-year teachers with additional activities is normal, but it happened. I will let you know if I drown or not."

Introduction

Some of the first questions I had before I started teaching were:

- How involved should I get with school activities?

- Should I volunteer for everything and risk having no time to plan lessons?
- Should I be selective, say "no" to a few things, and risk administrators being upset with me?
- While a first-year teacher knows he/she should get involved in the community, was there such a thing as too much involvement?

Without any experience to use as guidance, I followed the advice of others – and I'm glad I did. I will first discuss my apprehensions about saying "yes," and my potential room for improvement in the area. I will then address my successes in this lesson, how to manage the numerous responsibilities when taking on additional roles, and advice for incidents where opportunities are not presented.

Failures

Over the summer, before the start of the school year but after I was officially hired, my supervisor asked if I would be interested in being the junior class assistant advisor, a volunteer for a project for fostering culture, an after-school bus-duty employee, and a chaperone for a trip for the incoming freshmen class. This was all a few weeks before my first day. I was paralyzed with trepidation; I had no idea what the responsibilities for each role included. Feeling uneasy and nervous when being assigned to roles in which you are unfamiliar is natural, but it should not be overbearing.

Even though I had said "yes" to every requested role, my fears restrained my successes in these capacities. I spent too much time before my official start date, and during the first few weeks afterward, worrying about these small additional job roles. Furthermore, I also tried too hard striving for perfection with these roles, resulting in a huge time investment for job roles peripheral to teaching. Truthfully, other teachers and the administration do not take to these additional job roles too seriously. Of course, it depends on the assigned role, but typically, these additional roles should not be too time-consuming.

While I never said "no" to the administrators' requests, some teachers in my school did. While I could write pages describing my fellow colleagues' failures in this area, I will refrain from gossip. However, suffice it to say, it negatively affected them in regards to their relationships with students, administrators, and other colleagues. Student relationships suffered because students saw these teachers' lack of participation in outside activities as apathy. Consequently, teachers who refused to take on additional job roles had a more difficult time forming positive connections with students. Further, refusal may sever administrative ties with those teachers because it can create logistical nightmares for administrators. Administrators also prefer a teacher who demonstrates investment in the school community through taking additional job roles. Lastly, relationships with other colleagues were negatively impacted through rejecting additional roles because it created more vacant roles that other teachers needed to fill.

Some readers may argue that this lesson directly conflicts with Lesson 1, which warns against letting teaching consume one's life. How could one say "yes" to everything and still live a healthy personal life? This is a fair question, but I assure you that these lessons do not conflict, so long as you follow the upcoming advice. In the next section, I will discuss how I navigated these responsibilities.

Successes

This lesson originated from advice given to me by a teacher who used to work at my school. I want to first contextualize the introductory journal entry of this lesson. Four months before I started working for my school district, I was invited to view a student research symposium at the school. I was still a potential hire, and the administrators wanted me to see the culture of the school. While at the research symposium, I spoke briefly with Trevor, a teacher who led a portion of the symposium. I asked him if he had advice for a new teacher who would potentially be working with him at the school. Without hesitation, he told me, "Be a good soldier. Do everything they want you to do when you are young and able to do it. Make yourself valuable to the school." This was the advice I followed throughout my first year, and it served me incredibly well.

As demonstrated in the quoted journal entry at the introduction of this lesson, I took on many additional roles and promised that I would "let you know if I drowned or not." I did not drown. I took on all of the assigned roles – and more. Getting involved as much as I could was a huge asset for me: administrators liked it, I developed relationships that were more intricate with my students, and colleagues saw that I was invested in the school. Furthermore, and most importantly, doing these additional activities put a negligible amount of more work on me. That's right – the workload for these additional activities is hardly ever more than a mild annoyance. Even in the job roles that are infamously time consuming, there are ways to restructure the workload such that it becomes very manageable. For all my assigned roles, it took an average of about six hours per week to complete – that includes an hour of bus duty every day of the week. The net result is about six hours extra of work per week, and an extra five-to-ten thousand dollars on top of my salary for the extra work. That is a great deal.

There are, of course, caveats to this rule. Some new teachers may not be able to say "yes" to *everything* – I get it. Some first-year teachers may have other responsibilities to tend to, and cannot invest those few extra hours per week. I suppose the takeaway here is to say "yes" to as much as you possibly can, given your constraints. Do not feel apprehensive or nervous about the responsibilities, as they are often trivial and can typically be outsourced to students. In fact, students should be doing ninety-percent of the work in these roles. If you are running a club, have a student president responsible for the club's proceedings. If you are responsible for a student event, appoint or badger students for their assistance. Often, students feel honored by your request and trust, and they will skillfully carry out your requests. The biggest exception to this rule is coaching.

Coaching is always incredibly time-consuming and draining; use your own discretion here.

I found success in other areas of this rule too, which may be useful for the new teacher who has not been offered positions in the school community. After taking on, and being shocked at the manageability of, the other job roles I requested additional ones. Students were seeking a teacher who could run a concert, so I volunteered. I had never run a concert in my life, but I was confident in my abilities since the other roles went smoothly. I allowed the students involved to do nearly all of the work, checked in to make sure they were carrying out their plans, and watched the concert materialize. Because I ran the concert, they asked me to co-organize the school's biggest musical event – proactivity breeds further opportunities. I was proactive in other areas too. I, without being requested, sought to create a Critical Thinking curriculum with the Army's University of Military and Cultural Studies – something I had been interested in for years. I asked my supervisor about the feasibility of bringing in a former undergraduate professor to aid in our department's research goal. No matter if the request materializes, the simple act of requesting is beneficial. Despite my heavy involvement and proactive prospects, I could manage the additional roles with relative ease. This strategy aided me two-fold: administration noticed and appreciated my efforts, and students noticed and more constructive relationships formed. If no one asks you to fill additional roles, make sure to proactively request them.

Conclusion

If you are asked to take on additional roles at your new school, you may be worried about spreading yourself too thin – don't be. While it seems overbearing to manage the instructional side of the first year teaching along with the additional roles, I can attest that the additional roles are the least of your worries. If, for some reason, you are feeling overwhelmed with these additional roles, and you feel it is consuming your life (Lesson 1), then there are three options. The first, and something you should be already doing, is using students to lessen your workload. The second is to simply invest less energy into it; these job roles are peripheral to your main profession – you can slack a bit if necessary. If those options fail, the last choice is to resign from those additional roles. These roles are not important enough during your first year to sacrifice your personal life. Nonetheless, say "yes" to as many opportunities as possible. If administrators and/or students are not requesting you to take additional positions, start being proactive and seek out the opportunities. As a first-year teacher, you need to make yourself needed and noticed in the community. Saying "yes" to additional roles benefits your relationships with colleagues, students, and administrators.

THE TEACHING MIRROR

"There's a difference between trying to control students and establishing control of your classroom. Rules are about compliance. Procedures are about coherence."

- David Ginsburg

LESSON 3 – BE FEARED AND BE LOVED.

Journal on December 15: "I was looking through my old college history work to find something I could use for guidance on a research assignment I have to assign. I came across my old Machiavelli paper and PowerPoint presentation for my Historiography class – both assignments were trash. But Machiavelli's famous words rang in my head: it is better to be feared than loved..."

Introduction

Machiavelli stated that it is always better to be feared rather than loved. However, the question of whether to be feared or loved boils down to very different philosophies in teaching. The question essentially asks first-year teachers, "What type of teacher will you be? Will you be the strict authoritarian, or the lenient pushover? Will you raise your voice at students, or will you stand by passively?" While one's teaching persona exists along a continuum, it is best for teachers to take the middle route and sustain an arduous balance of being both feared and loved. I admittedly did not find much success in this area – I was far too loved throughout the year. However, my close colleague, Aaron, demonstrated the difficult balance to perfection. As such, I will first discuss my failures in this area and the consequences of those failures. I will then write about my limited achievements. Finally, I will address Aaron's successes, which I observed daily, and what I learned.

Failures

I am naturally endearing, somewhat non-confrontational, and relaxed. Even though these are desirable traits outside of the profession, allowing these personal attributes to seep into my teaching personality led to students "loving" me, but not "fearing" me. It is natural, I believe, for a new teacher to long for student admiration. However, this outlook – and the behavior pattern that follows it – spelled problems in my classroom.

Extending from my wish to have my students love me, I often refused to directly challenge problematic behavior or administer serious disciplinary actions. There was one class in particular where I let too much slide. In this class, I allowed students to be off-task and misbehave without any real consequence. Part of it was an experiment: how much learning was possible in an open and free classroom? Could students behave and learn if there were nearly no consequences? Would students learn more in this type of environment, or less? Of course, another part of it was that I wanted to these students to love me, and I was *very* loved in that class. Truthfully, that class was the most fun I had during my first year. However, it was not good teaching, and that was ultimately my job.

As a result of being loved, students started expecting me to do favors for them. Students began honestly admitting that they were not going to do certain assignments, speaking over me, going off-task, making jokes, and not doing the work. I handled these situations diplomatically and charismatically through humor or soft redirection. I do not want your image of the classroom as anarchy, as it was not. Though there were problematic behaviors, the class was fairly tame. Further, I also do not want you to think all of the students completely slacked off, as I had some of my brightest and diligent students in that class. Nonetheless, my use of humor and leniency illustrated to students that they could get away with certain things without actual penalty – and they acted on it when desired. I formed some of my closest relationships with students in that classroom environment, and the students absolutely loved being in a classroom that respected all of their comments and thoughts, no matter how off-task. I was adored in that classroom, and, while I cannot deny it was a lot of fun, it did not serve the students or me well.

Successes

I did find some success in this area. There were, at times, other teachers in the classroom working at their desks during my class (this was a normalcy at my school). As such, I was much stricter in those classes to maintain a particular image in the eyes of colleagues. While I still was not nearly strict enough, I noticed that students in the classes in which I was stricter respected me more, completed higher quality work, and had higher expectations for themselves. Furthermore, I felt that I had more control in the classroom. I could easily dictate when students spoke and when they stopped, when they worked and when they listened, and when they changed from one activity to another. While less fun than my previous class, the courses where I was in control gave me a glimpse of what "good" teaching looked like.

Aaron had demonstrated his incredible ability to be both feared and loved throughout the year – his secret was being consistent and being fair. Aaron was a master at this, and he called it being "strict, but warm." Aaron had an uncanny ability to be feared in class for certain things, yet loved for others. I will first breakdown his tactics for being feared and loved, and then go into the results of his actions.

In class, Aaron set concrete rules upfront for students. He had a strict no-talking-when-I'm-talking rule and another rule on always putting in one's best effort. Throughout the year, Aaron kept to these rules, no matter how confrontational or awkward it became. This is the key – consistency. There were several instances where Aaron would try to make an announcement to the class, and students would continue having quiet conversations on the side. Aaron would stop the class and escalate his intervention appropriately. The first strategy Aaron used was the stop-and-go technique. While students were talking over him, Aaron would start to make the announcement and then pause and look at the whispering students. He would repeat this two or three times before escalating the situation. If students continued to ignore his cues, he would say in an extremely stern voice, "Right now, I asked for attention, and you're not giving it to me. That sends a message of disrespect to me. When I ask for your attention, the expectation is that you stop talking, look up at me, and track me with your eyes so that I can see you are paying attention." Something like that line would typically shock the room into an awkward silence, but it would work wonders. In addition, to enforce his best-effort policy, Aaron would *always* be pacing about the room during student worktime and checking in with individual students. If it was evident that a student was not working hard, Aaron would say a similarly stern and clear message to the student individually that what they were doing was unacceptable, and that they needed to exhibit more effort. I want to make it clear that Aaron's tactics were extremely blunt, to the point, and clear; every student in that class knew when Aaron was unhappy with the class, or satisfied with the class. This level of firm communication kept students in a state in which they feared Aaron's wrath for not doing their best, yet simultaneously evoked a feeling of love for Aaron's fairness. Aaron also balanced those stern moments with many humorous jokes during class, which students loved. He would inject just enough to get a laugh, but then quickly move back to the material; he never let the humor continue rolling. Aaron also always went the extra mile, giving students personalized notes every quarter, and showing a true sense of caring towards students. This also promoted a feeling of love in students towards Aaron. Although I think

Aaron, at times, erred on the side of being feared, students also loved him; this formula ultimately culminated in respect.

Because of Aaron's actions in the classroom, I noticed a few interesting things. Students who were troublemakers, slackers, or hard-asses in other classes were respectful, hardworking, and cooperative in Aaron's class. I also noticed the culture in Aaron's classroom was one that craved respectfulness of others and genuine thoughtfulness. Students sensed and witnessed Aaron's rules, and acted accordingly. Through Aaron's receptive use of humor, students knew that they could have a little fun during class, but students saw that Aaron's class was for learning and working. I think this is in contrast to the class that I ran, as described previously, in which students saw the class as primarily a place to have fun with some working imbedded. Nonetheless, Aaron's results were impressive; he did not give up lovability for fear – rather, he established both through setting fair rules, clearly communicating them, and enforcing them fairly brutally. Yet, he also made it clear that his class was safe for joking, different perspectives, and thoughtfulness.

Conclusion

You may be tempted to become the cool, lovable teacher during your first year, or you may be tempted to lay down rules with an iron fist and be over-demanding. Both will not lead to many positive results. Rather, being both loved and feared leads to a teacher's greatest asset:

respect. To do so, carefully chose between one and three rules for your class, and be prepared to enforce those rules bluntly, sternly, and unsympathetically; those are the rules of *your* classroom, and do not let students break those rules. At the same time and equally as blunt and clearly, make students aware that little jokes and fun are allowed in your class, but be prepared to quickly refocus the class after these jokes. Humor in the classroom has a tendency to drag on or spiral out of control. Taking these steps will aid in achieving the delicate balance of being feared and loved. Attaining this balance should be a reaching aspiration for your first year, as it is extremely difficult to pinpoint that "sweet spot." Nonetheless, by being both loved and feared, you will foster the best in students, which will lead to both your and your students' successes.

"Teaching is a very noble profession

that shapes the character, caliber,

and future of an individual.

If the people remember me as a good teacher,

that will be the biggest honor for me."

\- A. P. J. Abdul Kalam

LESSON 4 – BRING POSITIVITY, ENTHUSIASM, ENERGY, AND MORALE.

Journal on October 18: "...I'll keep smiling and waving if they want me to. It feels a little demeaning in some ways, as if how well I can play politician determines my value. However, there are some aspects of it I enjoy. While I wish it were not true, only a portion of the enthusiasm is genuine. Don't get me wrong, I am grateful to have this job, but I am just so tired. Trying to seem full of energy all of the time makes it even more exhausting...."

Introduction

They did not hire you to be a good teacher. Yes, you read that correctly. As a first-year teacher, they expect that you will have instructional deficiencies – they do not expect you to be great out-of-the-gate. Though you must exhibit some proficiency at teaching, it is best to view your position as an investment; administrators believe you can become a great teacher with time and practice. New teachers must be forged by the harsh furnace of experience to become great.

THE TEACHING MIRROR

Like many new teachers, my primary concern during my first year was to be an effective teacher. However, it only took me about a month to realize that my primary concern did not match my superiors' concerns. As a new teacher, my administrators and my students did not expect me to be a tremendous teacher. Instead, I noticed that my administrators were scrutinizing new teachers on a different metric: the ability to bring morale through positivity and enthusiasm. While I found wide success in this area, I will first discuss my failures related to my wrongly placed emphasis on being a great teacher, rather than an enthusiastic and positive one. Then, I will outline examples of my successes, strategies for obtaining these successes, and the resulting effects.

Failures

I failed in this area on two separate occasions. The first was my inability to notice the importance of enthusiasm and positivity in the first few weeks of school. The second was my improper handling of a drama-filled situation between coworkers early in the school year. In both cases, I failed to bring positivity and morale to my colleagues.

During the first few weeks of school, I was so overly concerned with being a great teacher that I lacked some of the personable aspects that administrators wanted. Rather than introducing myself to all of my colleagues on the first day, I only introduced myself to my department. (I worked in my room the rest of the day, frantically preparing for the

Bring Positivity, Enthusiasm, Energy, and Morale

upcoming year.) Furthermore, as a fairly relaxed person, I did not bring in too much enthusiasm and/or energy into the school during the first few weeks. Again, my mind was spinning with the foreignness of everything – I was in no mindset to bring positive energy into the mix. I consider my actions a mistake, and guide others to bring in positivity, enthusiasm, and energy from the first day. If need be, fake it.

Another area in which I failed was my handling of a departmental clash between two colleagues. Within the first few weeks, my colleagues clashed on a manner regarding establishing growth goals. I will not gossip about the details here because that is precisely what I did wrong. I spoke to each of the colleagues in conflict about the situation, and oftentimes partook in gossip about each other. For example, in the beginning of the day, I would go to Coworker A, and gossip about the situation. Then, In the second half of the day, I would go to Coworker B, and gossip about the situation with them. I did not do this purposefully or consciously; I am just generally an agreeable person. However, I believe I did this in an attempt to win both coworkers over, but my actions resulted in both beginning to dislike me – and I do not blame them. Furthermore, the conflict between the two of them reached a school-wide-level gossip, and numerous faculty members started taking sides. Again, I started to play off other coworkers' views on the matter in an attempt to establish a bond. Though my antics created little damage, and any damage done was reversed later, it was an unneeded mistake.

Successes

After my disillusionment of needing to be a great teacher passed during the first few weeks, I began deliberately bringing enthusiasm, positivity, and morale to the school. Although I am regularly an introverted person, I definitely brought out my "performance" extraversions for my first year teaching. While my successes during my first year teaching may be limited, I did extremely well in this one area as the year progressed. I will first address how I brought positivity and enthusiasm, and the result of doing so. Then, I will provide advice on how to navigate "office politics."

There were many tactics that I employed to bring enthusiasm, positivity, energy, and morale – most of which may be obvious. I was consistently smiling in my class and in the hallways. I also made an active effort to remember the first names of all my colleagues, made small talk with them, and deployed as many of Carnegie's *How to Win Friends and Influence People* strategies as I could. While I certainly was not actively going out of my way to talk to people, I was conscious of always looking happy and being friendly, whether I wanted to or not.

The results of my efforts were stupendous. In the first week of November, the staff recognized me at a staff meeting – through an award system known as "kudos" at my school – for bringing morale. I also received personal visits by administrators, one in particular, who thanked me for the positivity and enthusiasm I was bringing to the school. Both examples were direct acknowledgements of my positivity and enthusiasm. However, there were subtle perks as well. For instance, administrators trusted me with the task of reinvigorating low-morale teachers through requesting that I work closely with them. It should be noted that administrators did not say, "Wow, you have such great energy! You should work with this teacher because he has low morale, and you can bring his morale up." (Though, admittedly, there were some conversations that I had with administrators that were equally as transparent). Rather, I could tell through their careful actions that my energy was a major factor in the logistical decisions they made. Administrators considered which colleagues I would be interacting with throughout the day when scheduling in an effort to boost morale where needed. Now, with my second-year teaching assignments already known, I can confirm that this point still holds true; administrators quietly and carefully place morale-bringing teachers in strategic positions. Being enthusiastic gives you value and makes you an asset to the school.

    I think the most difficult thing about bringing positivity, energy, enthusiasm, and morale is not that the tactics are difficult; it is that you simply do not feel like emitting them during the first year. You are so overwhelmed with the demands that bringing positivity and enthusiasm may be absent from your mind. However, you should view bringing positivity and enthusiasm as a high priority task included in your job responsibilities. Administrators realize that you are a new teacher who will need improvement instructionally. They also know that you will improve in the classroom over time and with professional development opportunities. However, even if you were the best teacher in the world, administrators would not be happy if you complained often, brought your colleagues down, and polluted the faculty culture. As such, one of your highest priorities should be to bring enthusiasm and energy, as those are what administrators are going to observe.

In regards to navigating drama within the school, one should be polite and aloof. Instead of participating in the gossip of the school, and damaging my relationships with both of my colleagues, I should have politely listened to each colleague's complaints about the other, but remained completely indifferent. I should have also avoided gossiping about the situation to other colleagues in the school. These things ruined the positive energy and brought morale down. Through politely listening to colleagues complain and/or gossip, you stay connected with them and are "in the loop." However, by refusing to participate, you remain neutral and liked by both sides. Remember that everyone knows everyone in education; the education network is small, and word travels fast throughout schools and across districts. If you gossip about the wrong people, or get a reputation for gossiping and bringing down morale, it will come back to hurt you professionally.

Conclusion

Your attention and concerns during the first few weeks of your first year probably involve instructional-related items. However, as a first-year teacher, it is important to know that administrators and others

Bring Positivity, Enthusiasm, Energy, and Morale

understand that you will not be a great teacher in the classroom. It takes years of experience and dedication to truly master the art of teaching. As a first-year teacher, they hired you to bring enthusiasm, positivity, energy, and morale. Administrators know that they can train a bad teacher to be a better one, but they cannot train someone to create positive relationships with colleagues, uplift attitudes, and improve faculty culture. You can bring morale in a myriad of ways, the simplest being to smile, greet everyone you see, use people's first names when speaking with them, and make small talk. Ideally, however, it would also be substantive to develop deep connections with those in your department and be a vehicle to help negative attitudes shift to positive ones. Furthermore, you should navigate the school gossip with care and caution; tune in, but do not partake. If you can do these things while surviving in the classroom, administrators will consider you a successful first-year teacher.

THE TEACHING MIRROR

"The art of teaching

is the art of assisting discovery."

- Mark Van Doren

LESSON 5 – REGULARLY EXPERIENCE GOOD TEACHERS.

Journal on August 14: "I have run into many teachers over the years. Many of them I have met through observations that were necessary for college courses, or simply because I had them in high school and I kept in touch. I have contacted my former teacher, who is now the assistant superintendent of the [redacted] School District, a prior observation teacher, and my previous student teaching supervisor..."

Journal on January 17: "...I'm so glad I am able to co-teach with Aaron. I honestly would have no idea what the hell to do if I did not watch him every day. It is somewhat weird – I noticed that I sound like him now. Like, Aaron has this unique inflection in his voice when he is speaking seriously. When he says "conversation" or "thoughtful," he puts these very distinct intonations in the word. Now, I'm doing the same thing without thinking about it..."

THE TEACHING MIRROR

Introduction

Teaching, itself, is a learning experience. As such, you should be open and willing to learn from great teachers at your school district. Working with a cooperating teacher during student teaching and a mentor teacher during your first year exposes you to some different teaching styles, but it does not substitute for regularly experiencing good teachers in the classroom. I will first briefly address my failures in this area, and my regretful lack of exposure to good teachers throughout my first year teaching. I will then discuss the excellent experiences I had when I took those opportunities and the value that they brought.

Failures

I want to briefly discuss the illusion that I, along with many new teachers, had coming into my first year following college and student teaching. Aspiring new teachers undoubtedly spend a lot of time observing teachers through college course requirements and working with cooperating teachers during student teaching. Because of the exposure to these experiences, some new teachers believe that they have solidified their classroom strategies and "teaching personality" before their first year even begins. I thought that I had most of it figured out before I started, which led me to be indifferent about watching other teachers in my school district. What could other teachers do so drastically different from what I had already seen? However, we can pick up bad habits from observing cooperating teachers and college professors, despite how great of teachers they often are. You absorb the style of the teachers you watch regularly – the good and the bad. In the sea of great teaching strategies that my cooperating teacher provided me during student teaching, there were a few areas where I obtained bad habits. I now regret not observing more teachers during my first year. There are great teachers at every school – seek them out and watch them teach.

There were three occasions where I observed other teachers in the building. My school district called it a "lesson ride-along" and teachers got professional development hours for partaking. While I will not claim these experiences as useless, I will assert that viewing teachers work in isolated samples does not yield much value. It was interesting to see how others teachers' classrooms functioned, but I never really grasped how they *actually* taught because I did not observe them regularly. It is extremely important to experience teachers on a regular basis so that you can get a concrete idea of how great teachers operate.

Successes

In the same manner that you absorb bad habits, you will learn good habits and observe creative ideas from regularly watching good teachers. Whether you are co-teaching the class or simply watching from the back of the room, if you regularly see good teaching, you will become a good teacher yourself.

THE TEACHING MIRROR

While I failed to observe many of the great teachers in my school district, I did co-teach a class with Aaron, who exhibited good teaching daily. As described above, prior to my first year, I had only witnessed my cooperating teacher and other college-required teacher observations and had adopted their teaching methods. However, when I saw Aaron teach, I realized how valuable watching other teachers could be. His methods were slightly different from what I had experienced previously:

- the way he structured his lessons down to the minute,
- how he interacted with students in a strict but warm manner,
- the way he showed students his investment in them via personal progress notes,
- how he navigated difficult behavioral situations through either humor or bluntness,
- how he asked thought provoking questions, and
- how he created meaningful assessments.

I found myself, oftentimes unwillingly, adopting some of Aaron's techniques in my own classes. I started to speak like him in class: clearly and concisely. I started organizing my activities like him through providing models, using the "I do, we do, you do" method, and setting timers. Above all, though, watching Aaron helped me see some of the bad habits that I had been unaware of before. For instance, I was not aware at how vague my directions were in class. After seeing how Aaron spelled out every expected detail for his students, I started doing the same. I also had a bad habit of mismanaging time and having loose lesson structure. After seeing Aaron, I started using timers for every class activity, and I comprehensively structured my lessons (see the slide on Lesson 18). I attribute these improvements to regularly observing Aaron teach. I hope that you too will seek to experience good teachers.

I would also suggest that first-year teachers reach out for advice from former good teachers and professors. Often, good teachers will provide first-year teachers with invaluable advice and veteran tips. I asked numerous education professionals, former teachers, professors, mentors, and friends for advice before and during my first year teaching. While much of it helped, there were a few pieces of advice that did not help. Be selective with who you ask for advice. Make sure you ask good teachers (for more on this topic, see Lesson 20). Though there is no substitute for physically being in a classroom with a good teacher on a regular basis, asking for advice can supplement the experience.

Conclusion

The teachers that you have been surrounding yourself with thus far, such as your cooperating teacher and others, may have been great teachers, but there is still an enormous amount to learn. To absorb good habits from great teachers, *regularly* observe a good teacher in practice. During your first year, make sure you ask around, through colleagues and/or administrators, about who the great teachers are in the building, regardless of the content. Speak with them, and

THE TEACHING MIRROR

make a determined effort to visit at least one of their classes on a regular basis. Through this, you will absorb and imitate their great teaching methods in your own classroom, and become aware of the bad habits you have already formed.

LESSON 6 – EMBRACE TECHNOLOGY.

Journal on August 23: "...Moreover, how do I contact the parents of my students? Should I contact them before school starts, welcoming them and their children to my class? Do I give parents updates on how their child is doing in my class...?"

Journal on September 14: "...I hate this Mac at school. I hate Apple products in general – they are just not intuitive for me..."

Journal on May 14: "...Luckily, I was able to copy literally everything from my school computer into a folder on Google Drive. That would have been a huge hassle to have to sort through it all and then email it all to myself or bring in a flash drive."

Introduction

Technology: a topic exhausted in college courses and teacher education programs. However, they often fall flat on demonstrating how to use it and the benefits/detriments of using technology in class. Perhaps you had an assignment once in a teacher education class to research some online tools, but the usefulness and practicality of those tools are questionable until tested. I hope to provide clarity as to the use of technology in classes through my experiences. I will first discuss my initial apprehensions and failures in regards to fully embracing technology. Then, I will outline my successes, strategies, and advice for new teachers.

Failures

I am fairly tech-savvy, and I received the typical college education course that centered on technology in the classroom. However, I was still skeptical of its uses. From my own experience as a student, technology seemed to distract students more than it aided them. In the school in which I student taught, the use of cell phones was almost entirely banned. However, my employer district had a relatively lax policy on technology, leaving most decisions up to the teachers' discretion. During the first few months, I shied away from using technology in the classroom out of fear of losing students to the ever-competing world of social media and the vast internet. My apprehensions, though, were mainly foundationless – it is just a matter of monitoring effectively. I will describe more about these methods in the "successes" section.

I also failed in accustoming myself to the technology of the school. I had used a Windows computer my entire life, and I had only used a Mac computer a handful of times. My employer district is an Apple-distinguished school, which means nearly every technology-related product was from Apple. As indicated in my September 14 journal entry, I was not a fan. For the first few weeks of my first year, I cowered into the only room in the school that included a Windows computer to get my work done. It was incredibly impractical, and annoyingly not connected to a printer. Working on the dated and unmaintained Windows computer also caused file conversion problems when transferring to my in-class Mac computer. I, eventually, got used to the Mac, but I rejected the operating system far too long. On the topic of Apple products, I had no clue how to work a Smart Board, and I still don't. I had one in my room, but I never used it. I can only imagine the instructional possibilities I wasted because of my rejection and fear of the new technology. I hope to learn more about its functionalities for the upcoming year.

Lastly, I did not use technology enough to stay in contact with families. Email and education apps make it incredibly easy to connect with parents regularly with little hassle. I only emailed parents when I received an email from them first, or when I was obligated to do so. This is an area where embracing technology would benefit you and your students' parents.

Successes

I learned, mainly from watching other teachers, that technology could be used to provide accessibility for students and create powerful lessons. I created an Edmodo page – an online educational social network that enables teachers to share content with students – for each of my classes, which allowed students to ask questions, access resources, and submit assignments whenever and wherever they pleased. It also enabled me to distribute materials without printing them. (There were more occasions than I care to admit where, because of the lack of time, I was unable to run to the copier and make copies. Edmodo was invaluable when in a pinch for distributing class materials). I also used technology to complement lessons. I allowed students to browse interesting websites, research current events, and discuss via comments on Edmodo. For instance, I – along with Aaron as my co-teacher – assigned an in-class activity where I gave the students the task to explain connections between industrialization and birthrates in different countries through exploring Gapminder, a site that aggregates country's statistics over the past few centuries. Another example within the same unit was an assignment in which students compared the level of industrialization of a given country with the quality of living through exploring a site called Dollar Street, which gathered pictures of mundane objects in nearly every country of the world. Both examples display how technology can produce an incredible learning experience.

Furthermore, I allowed students to use their own laptops, school provided iPads, or their phones in class. Most students elected to take notes on laptops for organization and legibility, and they usually respected their privilege and only occasionally went off-task. There are a few things to note to effectively use technology in the classroom. First, there must be some product that students turn in. If students have free time to "research," they will be checking their Instagram feeds instead. However, if students need to submit something, students will make sure to be on-task. Furthermore, technology has an attention-grabbing ability that disallows students to gaze up at you. If you want to speak to the class when students are using technology, you must request that they bend their laptops to a forty-five-degree angle, and turn over any phones or iPads. Otherwise, students will continue using their devices and will not hear a word you say. These tips stem from frustrating experience.

Additionally, I successfully used technology to organize my lessons and myself. Google Drive, Dropbox, and OneDrive are absolute musts to teach in the modern day. I had a folder for each unit in Google Drive, and then a Google Slides presentation format that I just copied and reused. It is also beneficial because students like familiarity, so having the same format slide is helpful. Every day, I displayed a slide that students would view upon walking into the classroom that contained the following information: unit number, objective, agenda, homework, and the do-now assignment. An example of the slide is below:

US I - Unit 3 - Lesson 3

- **Objective**: Students will be able to describe the controversies surrounding the Mexican-American War
- **Agenda**
  - Do Now
  - Notes (with video segment)
  - Documents Analysis
  - Closure Paragraph
- **Homework**
  - Chapter 13 Section 1 Outline due Friday @ 11:59pm
- **Do Now**
  - From yesterday's lesson and from the documents for homework:
    - Why did the United States go to war with Mexico?
    - Whose explanation for the U.S. going to war with Mexico do you believe more – that of President Polk or General Mejia? Explain your point of view.

Upon entering the class, students knew what assignment they should be working on, what the homework was, what the class activities would be, and the objective of the lesson. I started modeling this slide after what I had observed in Aaron's class, and it worked miracles. Gone were the nagging questions of "what are we doing today?" and "what's our homework tonight again?" I highly recommend using Google Drive and all its functions as it makes preparing and organizing class materials very easy.

While I did not often email parents, I succeeded when I did. Below is an email I sent to a concerned parent. While the content of the email is not important, there are a few things to notice.

Embrace Technology

> Hi Mr. & Mrs. [redacted]
>
> Ms. [redacted] kindly brought to my attention that you have been unable to access our classwork on Edmodo. Almost all of our homework assignments, many in-class assignments, and other updates are given through Edmodo. I will provide the classroom code for you below, and also invite both of you via email to join our Edmodo class. From this page, you will be able to see the homework assignments that are posted, and the attached readings that go with those assignments. I am also happy to email you our assignments if you would prefer; just let me know.
>
> Edmodo code: [redacted]
>
> Thank you, and please do not hesitate to reach out if you have any questions or concerns.
>
> Best
>
> Mr. Stanhope
>
>
> P.s. I have been working with [redacted] on our concert, and I am blown away at his guitar playing ability! I am really excited to see him perform at the concert!

The first, and the most obvious, is the professional aura and tone. You need to use common sense, but be extremely professional when speaking with parents — especially when emailing, as there is evidence in writing. More subtly, though, is the "p.s." message at the bottom. Despite having nothing to do with the situation, this part of the email is the most important. It establishes the bond between teacher and parent through the positive avenue of the child's talents. Whenever possible, include some form of the "p.s." message in all emails to parents. In other words, tie in a positive detail or observance about the student somewhere in the email. You will be astounded at the positive results.

Conclusion

Utilize whatever technology the school offers, and make the most of free-to-use online tools. Do not be apprehensive about using technology in many of your lessons during your first year teaching; simply make sure there is a presentable result from students to keep them on-task. In addition, I recommend obtaining students' attention through requesting that students put down their devices and their laptops at forty-five-degrees when you are speaking. I advise using Google Drive to organize your materials and expedite creation of new lessons through copying and editing already-made material. Furthermore, use an online platform, such as Edmodo or Google Classroom, to allow students to access materials outside the classroom and to assign activities inside the classroom. Lastly, make sure to contact parents on a somewhat regular basis, and use the "p.s." trick to ensure a positive interaction. Technology can create incredible learning opportunities and streamline your work. Embrace it.

THE TEACHING MIRROR

"Thirty-one chances.

Thirty-one futures, our futures.

It's an almost psychotic feeling,

believing that part of their lives

belongs to me.

Everything they become,

I also become.

And everything about me,

they helped to create."

- Esme Raji Codell

LESSON 7 – ACCEPT STUDENTS AS *YOUR* RESPONSIBILITY.

Journal on April 3: "...But that is exactly my job, isn't it? If a student is in my class, no matter how many issues he/she has, isn't it my job to make that student better? Isn't that student my responsibility...?"

Introduction

How much control do teachers feasibly have over their classroom? If you have had a student-teaching experience, how responsible did you feel for your students' behavior? How responsible were you for students' success? If a student misbehaved in your class, failed a test, or cut class, were you responsible for those actions? Or is it solely the student's responsibility? These are common questions for first-year teachers to grapple with, and questions that I, too, contemplated. The topic of responsibility is a source of heated debate among teachers; those who claim that it is the students' responsibility will be labelled callous, and those who claim it is the teachers' responsibility will be called masochists. My position on the issue should be no secret, given the title of this lesson – it is the teacher's responsibility. Accordingly, I will first present my failures of shifting responsibilities onto students and the consequences of doing so. I will then present my reasoning on the issue using my experiences with witnessing Aaron's class and my own class.

Failures

After student teaching, my undergraduate college asked for my participation as a panelist in answering aspiring teachers' questions. They asked me the following question: "What do you do when you see a student struggling in your class?" My response was to offer the student support, but I closed with, "Ultimately, it is the student's job to try and pass the class." I think most new teachers, and even the majority of veteran teachers, would see my response as fit and appropriate. However, I now see that outlook as shifting undue responsibility onto students.

There were many instances during my first year where I did not take responsibility for my students, especially when there was problematic behavior in the classroom. In fact, nearly every teacher I encountered refused to accept sole responsibility for things that occurred in their class. There were very compelling reasons to shift the blame. After all, teachers cannot control every behavior of a student in class, nor can teachers control how much time a student spends studying, or how many times a student participates. Teachers, perhaps rightly so, rationalize these undesirable behaviors as the students' responsibility.

In my experience, one particular case stands out in my memory. Early in the year, I had a student in one of my United States History I classes who was performing poorly academically but behaving well in class. I had heard that the student was having some family problems, and I sympathized with her. Nonetheless, I unpersuasively offered this student extra help a few times. When I failed to receive the students' homework and passively watched her plummeting test scores, I considered the matter the student's responsibility. I had offered extra help, and I believed that action to be good enough on my end. The student ended up passing the class with a D, but she did not improve throughout the year.

There were numerous other teachers, both in my employer district and in other districts I observed, who refused responsibility for their students as well. For the sake of privacy, I will only disclose general information. The most common indicators that teachers were deflecting responsibility were from their frustrated and irritated comments. Teachers might make comments such as, "Why won't these students just do the work I asked?" or "I have told students hundreds of times to stop talking while I am speaking; why won't they stop?" or "Why won't the students just study the review material I gave them?" Usually, these comments come from an endearing-yet-annoyed place. Teachers will believe that they have done their part, and now it was time for students to do theirs. In my recounted experience with the low-performing student, I followed suit. I told myself that feebly offering extra help was enough – I had done my part, right? The remaining onus was on the student to either inquire more about extra help, or try harder. These beliefs are only half-realities, and I will address those more thoroughly in the "successes" section.

The consequences of not taking responsibility led to apathy and indifference. Teachers typically stopped making the effort to redirect and correct student behavior through caring means. Moreover, teachers often mistook these situations as disrespect, which is partially understandable. Teachers believed students were ignoring or purposely defying their polite requests or slight offers for help. I observed some teachers get frustrated to the point of vengeance because of these misunderstandings. For instance, after numerous failed requests for students to complete their homework, perhaps a teacher may feel a pop-quiz is justified. Commonly, the conclusion is a cycle in which a student would behave undesirably, resulting in the teacher spitefully shunning the student or dolling harsh consequences, ultimately resulting in the student behaving undesirably again.

In my experience, I felt somewhat similarly indignant. Because I viewed my extension of help to a struggling student as enough, I sometimes thought that the student simply did not care enough about the class, or me, to pursue the extra help opportunities. Admittedly, this led to feelings of indifference towards this student for the first few months of my first year. When grading tests, I expected that student's grade to be low and felt it was justified. Because of this, I stopped making any additional efforts to help the student. Here lies the problem with putting the responsibility on the student. Whether teachers are actually responsible for students' performance or behavior in class is of limited significance – it is the teacher's outlook that matters. If teachers accept students as solely their responsibility, they are much more inclined to make continual and explicit efforts to redirect or help students. However, if teachers believe they have no real control over students' performance or behavior, they sometimes leave students to their own devices.

Successes

While I think the important aspect of accepting students as our responsibility is the mindset that follows, I also believe that teachers *can* control the performance and behaviors of students. Aaron had accepted students as his responsibility from the beginning, which led to his ability to control students' actions through setting a positive class culture. I want to discuss my experience witnessing Aaron's class, and then analyze my own classes in regards to how class culture, set by the teacher, can dictate student behavior.

Aaron and I had all freshmen in our Global Studies class. As freshmen, there were no preconceived notions about students' behavior or personalities, as I had not seen these students in any other situation or environment other than the Global Studies classroom. At my school, we have one day a week for after-school projects, where students can explore different projects run by teachers on nearly any topic for an hour. The freshmen, however, must attend a culture-building project during this hour, which aims to help freshmen students adapt to the rigor of the high school. I was one of the teachers who was involved in running the project, and I was able to see the students from Aaron and my Global Studies classroom in a new environment. I was shocked to see many of the students in our Global Studies classroom speaking while other teachers were speaking, joking around during independent work, and causing genuine problems in the project. How could this be? How could students be well behaved in one class but problematic in another? While there could be many different factors, I think the biggest one was the culture of the environment.

Students were high achievers and well behaved in Global Studies because Aaron had set a class culture that expected those attributes. Aaron accepted his role and responsibility for his students and demanded particular standards. He achieved this through demonstration, clarity, and rejecting misbehavior or low-quality work. From his candor, students felt somewhat fearful (see Lesson 3), and behaved in a way that mirrored the expectations and culture. Due to these factors, Aaron could control students' behaviors. If a student happened to hand in unfinished work, say something inappropriate, or misbehave, Aaron took that as his responsibility, and he took active steps to mediate or eliminate those behaviors. In effect, Aaron's mindset entrenched the idea that he could influence all aspects of his classroom, which led to him taking steps to improve it.

In my own experience, I could sense that the slight variations in my personality from class to class shifted how my students acted and performed. In the last class of the day, a class in which I felt prepared because I had already taught the lesson in earlier classes, I acted more thoughtful and raised my expectations. Because of this, my students in that class outperformed my other classes and were better behaved. My instruction was nearly identical from previous classes, but the culture I had set differed, which led to the positive changes. This taught me that I had a lot more control over students' behavior and performance than I ever believed. In the case with the low-performing student, I should have accepted the student's academic failures as my own teaching failures. I should have been more persistent and more concerned for the student. After all, teaching students is my job. It does not matter if a student is misbehaving, or performing poorly – it is *my* job to improve the student's behavior and academic achievement. If you accept that responsibility, you will take actions that will improve your teaching practice and student learning opportunities.

Conclusion

Many teachers believe they only have a finite amount of control in their classrooms and of students' actions, both academically and behaviorally. This is incorrect – or at least an incorrect outlook. Whether you believe it to be true or not, you must act as though bad students are nonexistent. Rather, your actions in class must parallel the mindset that all students have the potential to learn and grow with the proper assistance. Despite how frustrated you may get, you must ask yourself, "Is there something that I am doing to cause this behavior?" Perhaps students are not doing the work because you have created a particular class culture. Perhaps a student is not doing well because you have not explained it clearly to them. As the teacher, you can control the classroom culture through your actions, and you can control how students behave, achieve, or fail. Often, your students' actions are a reflection of you as a teacher; take responsibility for all students and their actions, and you will consistently be making improvements.

LESSON 8 – MASTER TEACHING, NOT CONTENT.

Journal on August 2: "...I have read a few books like Lies My Teacher Told Me and Why Nations Go to War in preparation for the year. I still feel like I do not know enough of the material to teach it – there is literally an endless amount of things to know. I think I'll read a few more books, maybe focused more on the US History I eras, and hope that it's enough..."

Introduction

One of my biggest fears before I started teaching was, "What if I get a class in which I am not confident in my knowledge about the subject?" As a history major in college, and now a social studies teacher, one would think that I would be extremely comfortable with the material. However, regardless of the field, this fear is common. Some topics were covered so long ago in college that our memory fades. In preparation for the school year, I started reading history books over the summer in an attempt to know everything about the history of everything; needless-to-say, it was neither practical nor helpful. What I came to realize throughout the year was that mastering the content is a separate, and often less important, entity from mastering teaching. I will first discuss my mistakes in regards to the overemphasis of content, along with common teachers' mistakes in the same area. Next, I will address what mastering teaching looks like, and why mastering teaching should take precedent over mastering content.

Failures

Perhaps it is a history teacher's ailment, but I was too invested in content before and during my first year teaching. As mentioned before, I hurriedly read as many class-content-related books over the summer to prepare for the year. I wanted to be an expert in the subject with the ability to answer all student questions regarding the content. It is certainly valuable to be an expert in your content. However, as a first-year teacher, it should not be a priority. Because of my quest to seek and obtain content information, my instruction suffered.

During my first weeks, I found myself structuring entire lessons around content. My class became more about knowing content, no matter how significant or minute the information, than about actual learning. Furthermore, I became incredibly pedantic with students, correcting every little content-related matter. These corrections on seemingly meaningless content yielded no beneficial returns. I sought credibility and authority from students through the corrections and presenting my vast knowledge in the subject – I got neither. Instead, I missed chances to actually practice *teaching*. I substituted engaging activities, creative projects, and student-driven exploration for dry, content-filled classes. Because of this, students and I both suffered; students didn't learn, and I didn't practice teaching.

Though my experience in this matter may be limited, I have seen many teachers and professors too focused on content. For those readers in or recently out of college, I am sure you have experienced a class where you learned little despite the professor being an expert in his or her area. If a class is not engaging, interesting, or interactive, it can be difficult to find the value and meaning that form genuine learning experiences. Even at my current school, there were teachers who were experts in their content area. Many held an M.A., M.S., or a Ph.D., discipline-related awards, and even patents. However, I saw no correlation between level of expertise and teaching ability. Students learned more in classes with teachers who could *teach*, rather than teachers who knew everything in the content area.

I must note that these assertions are not stating that content mastery is unimportant. It is always beneficial for students and teachers when the teacher is an expert in their respective content area. However, I will argue that teachers with sound teaching abilities and more limited content knowledge are more effective than teachers who only specialize in the content material. Therefore, especially as a first-year teacher, honing teaching skills should be prioritized over content acquisition.

Successes

The skills that first-year teachers should focus on are classroom management, clear delivery of instructions, proper assessment, and creating a positive classroom culture. This book delves deeper into all of these areas in other chapters, but the takeaway should be to focus on these areas over content. I quickly sought advice from Aaron after my content-focused lessons failed. As a teacher with masterful teaching skills, I studied his techniques closely to mimic them in my own classes. It was through Aaron's modelling that I was able to incorporate good teaching skills into my classes and improve student engagement.

To illustrate the sentiment of teaching skills over content, I want to describe one example in the Global Studies class that Aaron and I taught. There was a unit towards the end of the year on Japan, China, and the Koreas. Aaron had never taught anything related to Asian history, and he had extremely limited content knowledge on the subject. I, too, had an inadequate understanding of Asian history. Nonetheless, I witnessed Aaron pull together a tremendous unit using nothing but good teaching, general knowledge about Asia, and outside resources.

Aaron's good teaching came in the way of setting high and clear expectations, providing clear directions, and encouraging students to reach their potential. Aaron gave students the following assignment: using historical events, how did Japan, China, and the Koreas become what they are today? This was the overarching question for the unit, and Aaron allowed students to explore this question through readings, videos, and hands-on activities. Both Aaron and I were learning most of the material as we went along. When a student asked a question about a topic we did not know about, we simply admitted we didn't know and came back to it later. At the end of the three-week unit, numerous astounding class discussions orbited the central question. In these class discussions, students led small-group discussions that synthesized historical events with contemporary ones, offered plausible theories regarding the development of each country, and presented questions worthy of further investigation. The discussions were simply sensational. The success of this whole unit hinged on Aaron's teaching ability, not his content knowledge.

Ultimately, good teaching means effective student learning; and effective student learning means student engagement, discovery, exploration, curiosity, and understanding. A teacher with good teaching abilities finds ways to motivate students to discover the content and form meanings themselves. In this manner, a teacher need not be a master of content because students are the ones learning the content. I failed to realize this before my first year, and now it is a reality I embrace.

Conclusion

Typically, first-year teachers worry too much about their content knowledge. There is no doubt it is important, but being a good teacher is much more beneficial for you and your students. Teaching skills – which include handling behavior, providing clear directions, and establishing high expectations – must have a higher priority than content. Instead of cramming up on content before or during your first year teaching, make sure you hone your teaching skills first. Even the most knowledgeable experts in a field will make for a bad teacher if he/she does not obtain and refine their teaching skills.

LESSON 9 – REMAIN PRIVATE.

Journal on May 2: "...I overheard students saying they found out about a DUI case involving [redacted]. When I got back to my desk, I Googled it myself. I'm surprised [the teacher] hasn't tried to get rid of that..."

Introduction

Once something is made public, there is no taking it back. Especially in the age of the internet, everything is permanent. Though it depends on your level of comfort, I suggest being very cautious about what you share both to students and colleagues during your first year teaching. Gossip and judgement are both common with colleagues and students. I will first outline my failures in regards to imprudently sharing personal information with colleagues and students. Then, I will describe my successes and strategies for success for remaining private.

Failures

When it came to my colleagues, I got comfortable with a few of them and shared too much about myself. Although it took a few months, my colleagues became friends instead of professional coworkers. While this made for a very entertaining lunch period, it often hindered us from actually working during the school day during our preparation periods. More importantly, though, there were also some colleagues who weren't so friendly, and trying to befriend them led to workplace tension. Without getting into too much detail, this workplace tension was inconvenient and affected the culture among the staff.

I also mistakenly shared too much to students in class. While a certain level of openness is beneficial to form professional relationships with students, revealing too much to students lowers their esteem for you. In trying to relate to them, I shared my hobbies, my previous travel experiences, and some memories. Sharing these things is not inherently bad, per se, but it is best to keep most of it to yourself. Firstly, students seem more engaged and interested in teachers who do not share private details – teachers who are somewhat of a mystery. I have found that, even in my own experience as a student, students enjoy teachers of the unknown, rather than teachers who have shared it all. More importantly, though, is that you want to set a professional distance between you and your students. Sharing too many personal details might cause students to mistake you as a friend, especially if you are a young teacher. Therefore, I would recommend only sharing one or two things about yourself to relate to students.

Other teachers failed to maintain their privacy as well. I recommend that you Google your own name before your first year teaching, and get rid of any undesired search results. If it exists online, students *will* find it. This includes online profiles (yes, that includes dating profiles), court cases, forum posts, and any other imaginable medium in which your name might pop up. There were too many cases during my first year where students found their teachers somewhere online.

Successes

I did find some success in remaining private during my first year. I cleansed my online persona, and I became *much* more careful about what I shared to colleagues and students.

During my last year in college, one of my education teachers presented a PowerPoint with a slide that said, "What should I do about my Facebook profile?" The following slides consisted of embarrassing Facebook pictures of other students in the class. My professor had made her point: if she could find those pictures, future students could also find those pictures. In reaction to this powerful lesson, I took the interim prior to my student teaching and wiped everything clean. I changed my Facebook name, deleted old controversial posts, and removed any remotely contentious picture. I took aim at expunging everything that could potentially be traced back to my name. This paid off, as students searched my name on Google in an effort to find information about me. The only link that my students could find was my LinkedIn account – the only profile that remained because it was for professional use. It should be noted that, despite LinkedIn being a professional platform, students can still use it to find information about you. For instance, students found my age, previous work experience, hometown, and other personal details. I am unsure as to whether keeping my LinkedIn profile public was the right choice, but you should nevertheless be aware of the details that are on it.

Because of the negative results of befriending some colleagues, I became more inclined to not share personal details with them. It seems a bit disheartening, but I recommend finding two or three colleagues that you can consider trusted friends if you want to share any real personal information. You should view other colleagues outside this close-knit group as friendly acquaintances with whom you speak to and make small talk. This advice, however, is very subjective. Do as you wish.

Furthermore, I am more careful with what I share with students. One thing that I did very well, despite my failures mentioned previously, was that I never shared my political beliefs. As a social studies teacher, I think it is particularly important to show no bias with politics. However, I think it is a valuable lesson for all teachers. If your goal is to have a thoughtful classroom where you welcome different opinions, I think it is best to keep any bias quiet and allow for open discussions. This is one area where I earned respect from students; they saw me as levelheaded and a fair teacher who entertained and presented multiple perspectives. Related to politics, obviously do not share anything else that is controversial: religion, sexual orientation, personal belief systems and values, etc.

As a quick aside, aspiring teachers often ask me if they will be seen as the "new" teacher, and how to eliminate that stigma. The first answer is yes; both colleagues and students will label you the new teacher. However, there is luckily no real stigma for being considered new. Your colleagues will make some harmless jokes, and your students will be curious about you. Nonetheless, because you are the new teacher, colleagues and especially students will be prying to find out information about you. Again, be careful with what you share.

Conclusion

While this might be a more subjective lesson, I think first-year teachers should strive to preserve their privacy. Anything shared can be twisted, misunderstood, and gossiped about endlessly. Please take your privacy seriously, and be careful with what you share to both students and colleagues. For colleagues, I recommend you wait until you have formed a few close friendships at the school before you share anything too personal. For students, share only one or two things about yourself that highlight the best in you; sharing too much to students will lose you respect and authority. Moreover, keep any politics, values, and beliefs to yourself. Guard these heavily from students, as these are the few things that can actually get

THE TEACHING MIRROR

you in trouble. Lastly, make sure you delete all traces of you online. If it exists, students *will* find it.

LESSON 10 – BE SELF-AWARE.

Journal on December 2: "*...How did I not notice I did that? I am usually pretty self-aware with things, especially in situations where I am the center of attention. I probably have a ton of nervous ticks that I still have no idea about...*"

Journal on April 23: "*The shirt and tie thing is getting old. Speaking of which, I was giving a lesson today on Transcendentalism, and I had the 'Do Now' question as, 'Why do I wear a tie?' The point was to show that I wear a tie only because society says that a tie is professional – not because I actually want to. Students loved guessing the answer. A bunch of them were saying things like because I want to seem older, or because of a dress code. My favorite comment was, 'Because, unlike every other teacher in this school, you are professional.' Oh, how wrong he is, but it's funny how one extra piece of cloth fosters that perception...*"

Introduction

Self-awareness is the ability to consciously perceive your personality, skills, and actions. However, it is also the ability to recognize how others perceive you. While being introspective and reflective is innately part of teaching, being self-aware requires one to look even further beyond. It requires teachers to ask themselves, "How would doing x impact how students perceive me? How will wearing x affect how colleagues, administration, and students perceive me? When I said x in class, how did the students respond?" Being self-aware was a critical part of being successful during my first year teaching. I will first describe my failures in regards to my self-awareness instructionally, and common teachers' failures with self-awareness. Then, I will outline my successes in self-awareness with attire, and Aaron's successes with self-awareness in instruction and classroom management that I observed.

Failures

In my school district, each course must follow, more or less, the same instruction. This means that if there are three United States History I teachers, all of their classes should be nearly identical in regards to in-class instruction, grading, and homework. As such, I was inclined to follow what other teachers who taught the same course were doing in their class. This led to me assigning homework, projects, and assessments in which I did not have much of an influence in their creation. One such assignment was a weekly homework assignment that required students to read the textbook and tediously outline the text in a particular format. While outlining can be a useful skill, this assignment, I see now, was not meaningful. When my colleagues first presented the outlining idea, it originally unnerved me; I was not able to see the meaning in the assignment clearly. But, being a new teacher, I presumed my feelings were that of inexperience, and I assigned the homework without a word of disapproval. I never asked myself, "How will students perceive me if I assign these outlines? Will they respect the assignment and me? Or, will I lose respect, and students will view the outlines as a waste of time?" Instead, all of the teachers assigned the outlines with limited modelling and examples, and only providing students with a brief description of what was expected. Reflecting on it now, the results were predictable. Students complained about the assignments, failed to take them seriously, started cheating, plagiarized, and ultimately got little out of it. Because we were not self-aware with our assignments, my colleagues and I lost some of our students' respect.

Another quick example of my lack of self-awareness, and the astounding ability for students to notice your every action and/or inaction, is my gum-chewing habit. I chew a lot of gum throughout the day, but I never thought that students would notice my habit. On the last day of school, while students were giving teachers small gifts, a few students gave me packs of gum. It blew me away; how did students notice that little habit? While it did not negatively affect me, it is just another anecdote to demonstrate how important it is to be self-aware, because people – especially students – notice everything.

I also failed to be self-aware with a strange nervous tick of scratching my head in class. This had more to do with the lack of confidence, and so I will expand further on this in Lesson 13. However, it is worth mentioning here because, as a first-year teacher, you will most likely have some sort of quirk of which you are unaware too.

Lastly, the most common area where teachers are either not self-aware or apathetically self-aware is their attire. Many teachers arrive to work dressed casually in jeans and a t-shirt. These teachers may ask themselves, "How will others perceive me if I wear a t-shirt to work?" Their indifference regarding the answer to that question is problematic. While nothing but a few sly comments from students, jokes from colleagues, and disapproval-filled glances from administrators typically occur, it is best to simply dress professionally. As a first-year teacher, you *must* dress professionally on a daily basis.

Successes

Despite some of my failures to be self-aware in regards to my instruction and assignments, I was very self-aware in my attire. Furthermore, I want to highlight Aaron's self-aware in instruction to provide readers with concrete examples in the area in which I failed previously. I will quickly discuss these two examples, and then expand on other topics about which you should be self-aware.

Be Self-Aware

I was very deliberate and borderline obsessive with my attire. Every day, aside from Pep Rally Day and Field Day, I wore slacks with a dress shirt and tie: no exceptions. I was very self-aware, and asked myself before the school year started, "What attire will make others perceive me as a professional?" This is an especially important question for young first-year teachers. I obtained a reputation as the teacher who *always* dressed up. Having that reputation alone is worth the weekly ironing and daily tie tying. This reputation pleases administrators, communicates authority and integrity to students, and my colleagues generally liked it. One caveat is to not overdo the dress, as colleagues might see you as "that teacher" who is trying too hard and making other teachers look bad. In other words, do not wear a suit, but look professional all the time. (As a quick aside to prove the importance of self-awareness, my dress pants got looser and looser over the course of my first year; I lost about 20 pounds during the year because I was making weight for jiu-jitsu competitions. Because of this, I had to continually up-notch my belt until the last hole. By the end of the year, my slacks still looked good and professional, but they were slightly malformed due to the tightness of the belt. On the last day, I got an anonymous note through a student survey that jokingly requested that I get pants that fit me. This is to reiterate that students will notice everything, so make sure you notice it too and then act accordingly.)

Furthermore, Aaron was incredibly self-aware with instruction. As opposed to passively submitting to what other colleagues were doing, Aaron would often express his disapproval of seemingly make-work assignments and/or sometimes deviate from colleagues' instructional plans to create a more meaningful lesson. It was not typical school procedure to have two teachers who taught the same course doing separate things in class, but Aaron's commitment to worthwhile instruction surpassed these procedures. When brainstorming some instructional thoughts with Aaron for Global Studies, Aaron often rejected ideas with the question, "Could you imagine *me* doing that? Do you see what kind of message that sends to students?" Essentially, Aaron was being self-aware and asking himself, "What kind of teacher will students perceive me to be if I assign this? How will their respect and/or esteem for me fluctuate?" Through this, Aaron's self-awareness created better instructional outcomes for students.

Aaron was also self-aware with his classroom management. Throughout the year, I asked Aaron numerous situational questions to see what his answers would be, and his responses were always filled with self-awareness. Aaron also modelled those management skills in class during our Global Studies class. For instance, if a student whispered while Aaron was speaking, Aaron would call out that student *every time.* If Aaron described instructions, which were always crystal clear, and a student then asked a question which had already been explained, Aaron would refuse to repeat himself *every time.* If a student took a class discussion off-task, even acutely, Aaron would explicitly refocus the conversation *every time.* When I asked him about these situations, or others, Aaron's responses were always identical. Aaron would say, "What kind of message are you sending if you don't act every time?

How would students perceive you as the teacher? How would that affect the classroom culture?" Aaron's self-awareness regarding his management and actions in the classroom created a classroom culture in which students respected Aaron, knew the expectations, and worked hard.

While classroom management, instruction, and attire are all very important avenues in which to practice self-awareness, you should also be mindful of other areas as well as a first-year teacher. Self-awareness is a means to build a reputation. As such, if you are wondering what you should do in any given situation, consider the following question, "How will administrators, students, parents, and colleagues view me?" Ask this question to promote self-awareness, and it will solve numerous issues quickly. For instance, if you are wondering whether to bring students to the computer lab for an assignment, ask yourself the question. Your answer might be, "Administrators might view me more positively for incorporating technology, and students might view me as engaging because they like working on computers but they also might become off-task. Parents are not a significant player in this decision, and colleagues might view me as a computer-lab hog." Therefore, you should plan your actions according to your answer. You may conclude that you should go to the computer lab to incorporate technology, be very clear with expectations and strict with off-task behavior from students, and be sure to check with colleagues to make sure there are no potential reservation conflicts. Through asking this question, and being self-aware, you can generate actionable solutions that promote a positive reputation to every new situation that arises.

Conclusion

Self-awareness affects numerous topics, such as attire, management, instruction, school event participation, faculty relationships, and much more. To ensure that you are building the best possible classroom environment and reputation, you must act on the new insights from your self-awareness. An easy way to promote self-awareness is to ask yourself the question, "How will administrators, students, parents, and/or colleagues view me?" Your answer will clarify your best options for any decision.

LESSON 11 – ANTICIPATE THE UNEXPECTED.

Journal on September 22: "…At least there haven't been bomb threats yet, like there were in my student-teaching school district…"

Journal on October 21: "That backup plan saved me today. I thought this historical analysis activity would take the majority of the period, but it only took like 10 minutes. Maybe the students lazily completed it. I'm still not convinced they could have done it that quickly. Whatever. The good news is that I had something to fall back on, especially with [another teacher] in the room. I looked like an idiot who had no idea what he was doing, which I am. But, I would have looked like an <u>incompetent</u> idiot who didn't know what he was doing if I didn't have that backup plan…"

Introduction

In my college classes, my professors would always advise to anticipate students' questions and sources of confusion within the material. This is, obviously, good practice. However, a teacher should anticipate problems that may occur in many other areas. I had to learn from experience of three areas where first-year teachers need to anticipate the unexpected: emergencies, lesson/unit planning, and job stability. I will address each of these with my own failures. Then, I will offer my solutions in the success section to avoid these failures.

Failures

I failed at anticipating the unexpected too many times throughout my first year. However, I am now much more prepared to handle those unexpected occurrences. These failures in the three areas listed above will illustrate situations you may find yourself in as a first-year teacher.

The first area where a first-year teacher must anticipate the unexpected is in emergencies or, more likely, emergency drills. During my orientation, my school district briefly went over the procedures for fire alarms, lockdowns, and shelter-in-places. With all of the other things pedaling in your mind during your first few days on a new job, these procedures do not stick. Most of my classes were in a room that I shared with Aaron, and it was also his first year at the school district. Thus, when that first shelter-in-place drill occurred, Aaron and I both looked at each other, hoping that the other remembered the plan. We did not. Fortunately, we were able to reasonably guess the procedures. Nonetheless, it was anxiety inducing, and a situation that could have been avoided. Furthermore, during one of the first fire alarm drills, I recall I had an off period, so I just walked outside towards the throng of teachers and students. While outside, I was speaking with a coworker of mine when one of the supervisors walked over and asked my colleague, "Do you have all of your students?" My colleague gave an affirmative head nod. When the supervisor left, my colleague said he had no idea if he had all of his kids. These two experiences, along with other minor experiences punctuated with fleeting moments of unease and fear, led me to start planning for these potential drills and emergencies

Another area, and probably the most expected "unexpected" issue that a teacher must plan for, is unaccounted-for time during class. This is a common problem for first-year teachers, and it was for me too. I had one instance during student teaching where a lesson ending in half of the time than I had anticipated, leaving me with half of the class period with nothing to do. I remember my cooperating teacher's advice, which was to have extensions for every lesson. This worked in the short-term, but once I got into my first-year teaching, there was simply too much to do. I couldn't plan lessons *and* extensions that may or may not be used in class. I reverted to just hoping my plans worked out and, to my surprise, they did most of the time. However, during one fateful day when it did not, it was nerve-wracking – *very* nerve-wracking. The emotions that a first-year teacher feels during those waning moments of the lesson, where the teacher knows that he/she is running out of things to say or activities to do, and there is still a sizable chunk of class time remaining, are poignant. I recollect when I had students doing a document analysis activity on the American Revolution – something I thought would take twenty-five minutes – took only ten minutes. I had fifteen minutes left of class time and absolutely no plan. Thinking quickly, I told the students that they could work on their homework outlines. I knew they would not, and they could easily sense that I had mistimed the lesson. Moreover, my request that students work on their homework was conspicuously superficial, as many students did not have access to the needed material to complete it. This was an embarrassing incident that persuaded me to find a solution, and plan for the unexpected.

    Lastly, a first-year teacher should be mindful of the ultimate unexpected: job stability. During my first year, I was so engulfed in trying to make materials, answer emails, and form decent lessons that I never considered the potential for being fired or not being rehired for the following year. Despite the constant jokes from my mentor teacher that I would not be rehired, I never actually considered the possibility, nor my plan of action if it occurred. Throughout the entire year, I did not update my résumé, LinkedIn, or seek potential future employment opportunities. It was not until mid-April that I actually thought about the chance that they could let me go. While I, thankfully, was re-signed for another year, a first-year teacher – and all non-tenure teachers – should take steps to ensure their continued career, with or without the current school district.

Successes

While college courses may address the mistimed lesson incident, the other two areas are typically overlooked. Accordingly, I want to describe my solutions to these happenings – solutions that proved successful by my experiences.

To be prepared in an emergency drill or otherwise, a first-year teacher should take a few precautions. First and most obviously, make sure you know the emergency procedures. You are liable for what occurs, especially if you breach provided guidelines. Because Aaron and I could not remember the procedures during the first drill, I created a small print out with an abbreviated list of steps for every situation/drill. For instance, on this print out, I had "fire drill," and then bulleted notes that said:

- *Out the door to the left*
- *Close door*
- *Turn off light*
- *Take attendance*

I have one of these for each possible drill, and it took ten minutes to create. Now, during any drill, I simply look at this sheet and follow the steps. Another important trick that I learned from my experience previously described with my colleague, where my supervisor asked him if he had taken attendance, was to always keep an "emergency folder." I kept this folder on top of a cabinet in the room so it was easily accessible during drills and emergencies. This folder also contained a copy of the bulleted instructions, but more importantly, it contained a roster for every class I taught. This way, I could take attendance once my students were outside. With these few tricks, I was able to feel prepared for the unexpected emergency.

In regards to unexpected lesson-timing mistakes, the best way to mitigate these situations is with a unit plug-in or an ending activity. After my mishap, I sought advice from a former teacher and current assistant superintendent. I described to him my struggles in this area, among many others, and he explained that mistiming lessons is extremely common, and there are two ways to navigate the issue. The first option, which is especially useful when you are unsure of your timing estimates, is to have an ending activity that has no constituted time dedication. For instance, the ending activity could be for students to write a paragraph using as many vocabulary words as they can from the day's lesson, it could be a review game, or – if appropriate – it could be students working on their homework. These closure activities have the potential to last the remaining class time. The other option is a unit plug-in. In this choice, the teacher develops one "backup" lesson while designing the unit as a whole. The "backup" lesson is designed such that it could technically fit anywhere within the unit and be workable. For instance, if a teacher was designing a unit on the Vietnam War, then the teacher might have a "backup" lesson on the similarities and differences between the Vietnam War and modern-day war tactics. If a situation arose where a teacher ended a lesson on the Vietnam War early, the teacher could implement this "backup" lesson and transition to another activity. When considering "backup" lessons, it is important to do three things. First, make sure the lesson can reasonably fit anywhere within the unit. This is the most difficult part, but as long as it somewhat fits, it should be workable. Secondly, make sure the lesson is in a folder somewhere memorable. I keep my "backup" lesson for each unit in my top drawer; it would be incredibly unfortunate to prepare a backup lesson and then forget where you put it when you needed it. Lastly, make sure you prepare any copies or materials beforehand and place them in this folder. This "backup" lesson plan strategy has gotten me out of trouble twice, and it is worth doing just to have the insurance and peace of mind.

The last piece of unexpected territory that first-year teachers must prepare for is job stability. While it may sound disheartening, some teachers are not rehired for the following year. Typically, you have no real worry about them terminating you, as most contracts state that teachers must have sixty days' notice. However, you must worry about not being rehired. Upon my realization that they may not rehire me, I updated my résumé, LinkedIn profile, and refreshed my employment opportunities. In regards to the updated résumé, I included anything that I accomplished over my first year. However, I also transferred my résumé into a business résumé, just in case I had to apply for non-education-related jobs out of desperation. To do so, "collaborating with colleagues in an inclusive classroom to ensure students' needs were met" became "collaborated in a team environment with colleagues and clients to ensure optimal results were obtained." In essence, I altered semantics to align more with the business world. In regards to seeking new employment opportunities, I browsed the new teaching jobs posted weekly. In fact, before I knew if I was going to be rehired, I actually applied, interviewed, and nearly demoed a lesson at another school district. Fortunately, I got the news that they were rehiring me before the demo was necessary. However, if for some reason I was not going to be rehired, I had a backup plan and had already been looking. This piece about job stability may be a bit too future-minded for first-year teachers looking for advice before the school year starts; but hopefully this advice will remain in your mind so that, come March or April, you may prepare for the worst-case scenario.

These are the solutions that worked for me. While the solutions are elastic, the problems are unchanging. If you do not use my solutions or create a suitable replacement for yourself before the year starts, you *will* run into the same or similar situations as I did. I recommend you take some time to consider how you will prepare for the unexpected in these three areas, write down your responses, and take action from your first day.

Conclusion

Teaching requires one to be flexible when the unexpected occurs. However, some unexpected events are more predictable than others are. The three unexpected areas that I wish I had prepared more for were emergencies, lesson time mismanagement, and job stability. To ameliorate these problems, you should either enact my solutions or create your own. For emergencies and drills, I recommend making a bulleted list of faculty procedures. For class mistiming, I suggest either an ending activity or a unit "backup" lesson. Lastly, I advise you to update your résumé throughout the year and browse for potential future employment opportunities. Be more prepared than I was.

THE TEACHING MIRROR

"In an effective classroom,

students should not only know

what they are doing,

they should also know

why and how."

- Harry Wong

LESSON 12 – SET CLEAR EXPECTATIONS.

Journal on December 11: "...Marking periods are such a nightmare. This one, with winter break, is especially bad. The test we gave in USI went terribly – students were complaining even before they took it because of what they had heard from their friends about it. I input the grades today before saving them to see the damage done: it was pretty bad. I'll have to talk to the other teachers about a curve so that we don't destroy kids' grades and get them grounded for the Holidays."

Introduction

As a student, I always hated surprises. As a teacher, I hate them even more. This is not to say that we should avoid fun, surprising hooks to introduce class, or swift mid-lesson alterations – quite the contrary. However, it is very evident that students prefer routine and clarity when it comes to expectations. There are, however, many avenues in which new teachers should seek to set clear expectations. I will discuss three separate areas where new teachers need to be mindful of setting expectations: classroom procedures, grading requirements, and end-of-marking-period grades. The first two aspects are typically discussed in college-level education classes. However, using examples helps clarify the vague concepts typically used in college courses. Furthermore, the last area is rarely mentioned in college classes, and one that is extremely valuable. I will discuss my failures, successes, and tips for first-year teachers in each of these three areas. I cannot overstate the importance of this lesson. Setting *clear* expectations is the difference between a good teacher and a great one.

Failures

As a new teacher, I "knew" to set clear expectations and to create rubrics for assignments, but what did these things actually look like in the classroom? The extrapolation into these areas in college was usually ambiguous and lacked lucidity. As a result, I made numerous mistakes in these areas. Further, I also made a huge mistake in end-of-marking-period grading.

In regards to classroom procedures, I generated a set of expectations from my cooperating teacher, which were developed during student teaching, along with advice I had read in articles on the internet. The expectations I adopted included three requirements for students: show up, try, and be nice. This is what I told my students during my first class. As long as they showed up, tried, and were nice, they would be successful. In some ways, it was true. In other ways, it was setting very low expectations. Students acted accordingly; they would show up to class, give some effort, and be pleasant. However, after I had found my footing after the first month or so, I realized that the quality of work from my students was fairly low. The class discussions were lackadaisical, they completed their homework assignments in an ostensibly rushed manner, and students would often be distracted during independent work in class. It took me a few weeks to realize that students were doing exactly I expected of them – nothing more. I had set and enforced these expectations since the first day, and so students took the path of least resistance, putting in *just* enough to meet the expectations. They showed up, but were sometimes late. They tried, but put in minimal effort. They were nice, though; I have no criticisms here. Nonetheless, because I had set these expectations, students acted in accordance with them.

I also made mistakes with grading requirements through rubric making – or lack thereof. Even when I did create rubrics, they were sometimes unfair. I failed this lesson with respect to rubrics in four areas: projects, class participation, homework assignments, and class discussions.

During my first month, there was a project given in the United States History II class in which I was a collaborative teacher. The assignment consisted of students roleplaying significant American historical figures during the Spanish American War. When students asked for grading details, the answer that both the other teacher and I gave was that we would grade the quality of the discussion and the historical accuracy. Students, slightly displeased, accepted the answer. When the students finally present their projects, the grading seemed random – and I was one of the people grading it! My colleague and I were both grading the students, but we did not know what to look for during the conversations. What made a "quality" conversation? Was it that there were no silences? Or perhaps that they all spoke an equal amount of time? I arbitrarily gave each group a grade based on how I felt it went. When my colleague and I went over the grades for each group, we sometimes had very different grades. I imagine several students received their grade and asked themselves, "Why? What else was I supposed to do?" This type of grading that involves unclear guidelines, such as "quality of conversation," is surprisingly common, and leads to students forming an external locus of control, since they feel no control over their grades.

While I self-corrected this quickly, I originally failed at my development of rubrics for class participation. This is also a very common fault in first-year teachers' grading systems. I adopted my former cooperating teacher's system of grading class participation, where I gave students a biweekly grade based on their perceived participation. Like during student teaching, I gave the highest grades to those students who raised their hand a lot, and low grades to quiet students. This system is controversial, as there is a large possibility of a quiet student being just as engaged as an outgoing one. Regardless if this is true, this grading system was flawed because it neglected the majority of students. It was easy for me to know who the two or three outgoing students were, as they participated numerous times per class. It was equally as easy for me to know who the five quiet students were, as they never participated. Grading these eight students was trouble-free. But what about the other twenty students? Sometimes they participated, and sometimes they didn't; how would I grade them? Using this arbitrary system, I simply guessed. Some students would get a B, some an A-, some a B+, because I "felt" that they should have that grade for participation. There was no objectivity, and it led to students being confused and surprised at their class participation grades. Due to the problems I had with this, I stopped giving class participation grades after four weeks.

Moreover, I also failed at using rubrics for homework grading. As mentioned previously, nearly all homework assignments in my United States History I class consisted of outlines, where students would read and outline the textbook. They completed these outlines in pairs, and each outline would typically be between five and twelve pages per pair of students. A rubric was created for grading these outlines, but it was incredibly vague and, honestly, I never used it. Nonetheless, there were two flaws with these homework assignments in regards to rubrics (there were many non-rubric-related flaws to these homework assignments as well). The first is that students were working in pairs, and it was often difficult to see precisely where one student's section ended and the other student's began. I instructed students to use different fonts or colors to differentiate between their works, but it was sometimes problematic. Furthermore, having students work in pairs created a situation where I would be comparing the two students' work with one another. For instance, I would say

"Well, Student A's outline looks a bit more organized than Student B's. I guess I will give Student A a slightly higher grade than Student B." It did not matter if both students did a great job; one student would typically get a slightly higher grade. The second flaw, and the most drastic, was that these outlines were given multiple times per week. This means that I would have close to one hundred pages of outlines to grade per week. This is simply not feasible. It became an assignment that I graded with instances where I would simply take a quick look at it, and move on. This, again, led to student confusion over their grade. How could I justify their grade if I did not read it thoroughly? These became a major source of student complaints – and I do not blame them.

The last area of rubrics in which I failed was class discussion rubrics. I spend a great deal of time trying to perfect Socratic Circle, Fishbowl, and Harkness discussion formats in my classes. These were always a source of excitement for both students and me, and I would recommend any new teacher implement them into the class. However, the grading system that I used created some negative surprises for students. As I was taught in college, the traditional Socratic Circle and Harkness discussion grading systems relied on teachers grading the class as a whole, as oppose to individual students receiving their own grade. The idea is to motivate the outgoing students to encourage the quieter students to participate. However, the outcome is typically that those students who have not done their prep-work and the nonparticipating students pull down the more participatory students' grades. And vice versa, the students who were not prepared or did not participate received higher grades because of those students who did participate. The result was grades that did not reflect the students' true efforts or actions. When students received their grade for the discussions, many were frustrated and confused.

Lastly, I created several problems through shocking students, and their parents, with the end-of-marking-period grades. It is almost customary for teachers to assign unit tests, large projects, or other forms of assessment that heavily influence students' grades at the end of marking periods. When the end of the marking period was nearing, there was always a unit test in my class to complement it. During my first-year teaching, I gave a unit test towards the end of the second marking period. I am not sure if it was the test itself, or some other factors, but students did not do well. While there was a slight curve on the grades, most students did a letter grade or two below their average work. Being a unit test, it was worth a significant amount of points in comparison with the rest of the grades for the marking period. This resulted in students, having done well throughout the second marking period and had been receiving an "A" up until the unit test, getting a "B-" in their gradebook. Because it was the end of the marking period, students knew they could not make their grade up using future assignments. Parents, especially, were concerned; they have been habitually checking their child's grade for weeks and it all seemed fine. Now, in the last few days of the marking period, their child's grade dove sharply. Parents rightly demanded answers, and I had a lot of explaining to do. This mistake was disastrous, especially because it involved parents.

Successes

The keys to avoiding these failures are to set *clear* expectations, create detailed and objective rubrics, and to plan ahead with your units. I want to describe solutions to the three areas in which I failed during my first year: classroom procedures, rubrics, and the end-of-marking-period grading. While I have written about Aaron's expectation strategies previously, I will detail them more concretely so that others can imitate his methods. Furthermore, I will include Aaron's strategies with creating rubrics, as he was definitively the best at it at our school. Lastly, I will share my strategy for avoiding troublesome end-of-marking-period grading situations.

Aaron established clear expectations. His literal words were, "You are expected to," followed by the exact high expectations he wanted. For example, before having one of our class discussions, Aaron said, "You are expected to be extremely thoughtful with your comments. Think about what you want to say, how to best say it, and how it will affect others before you actually say anything." Unpacking this, Aaron essentially told students that they needed to be thoughtful, articulate, and mindful of others during conversations. He consistently stated these expectations before any activity or project. However, Aaron's success perhaps came more from his constant, sometimes harsh, upholding of those expectations. For instance, using the discussion example above, if a student were to say something off-topic, ill constructed, or even remotely mean-spirited, Aaron would call it out in no uncertain terms. There was one instance during a class discussion in which a student said something off topic, and Aaron's reaction was, "Okay, that added nothing to the conversation and was not meaningful." While this is an unusually harsh example, I use it to illustrate that Aaron had no problems with making students feel uncomfortable or even slightly bad if they did not meet his expectations. Aaron also used something called "Criteria for Success." The "Criteria for Success" would be a two-to-five bullet-pointed list that served almost as a checklist for students. Aaron would say, "If you have done these things listed under the Criteria for Success, you will be successful." For instance, Aaron assigned an exit ticket that directed students to write a paragraph that took a stand on the following statement: The United States should intervene in the Rohingya crisis in Burma. On the board, the "Criteria for Success" read, "Include a well-developed thesis, use three examples to support your reasoning, and connect this crisis with another crisis in history." If students did all of those things in their exit ticket paragraph, and did them well, they would be successful. This made the expectations extremely clear, and students had no confusion as to what was expected of them. Like in my classes previously described, students acted accordingly, and would unswervingly meet Aaron's high expectations. There were no surprises; if a student went off topic or made a half-thought-out comment, it was expected that Aaron would step in authoritatively.

Expectations heavily overlap rubrics, as rubrics detail the expectations for students on assignments. The remedy for numerous problems regarding rubrics comes in the form of abandoning them; you simply cannot have a rubric for *every* assignment in class. My problem regarding the outlines was that I attempted to use a rubric on homework assignments that should not have had one. Instead, due to the sheer volume of work, I will switch to a complete/incomplete homework grade next year. If I cannot give my time to read all of them, I cannot grade them on a rubric scale. A complete/incomplete will allow me to quickly glance through the homework and give a fitting grade. This type of grading is more suitable with the most forms of homework assignments. Similarly, the remedy for class participation grades was to abandon the rubric. It simply did not encourage students to participate authentically, and the grading was too random. By removing the grade, students participated through genuine means, there was no arbitrary grading, and I did not have the responsibility to track how often students participated.

Obviously, abandoning rubrics only works when the assignment does not fit a rubric model. Assignments like class discussions and projects still need rubrics; they just need to be well done. Aaron was great at creating rubrics; in fact, he was neurotic with rubrics. He wanted to ensure students knew the grading system, and the rubrics were detailed and thorough. In doing so, he made strict-yet-clear rubrics that made even the most subjective things, like class discussions, objective and inclusive of individual accountability. For one class discussion in Global Studies, he created a table to show students how he was grading them. The chart and his explanation detailed that each student must participate in the class discussion three times, and each time he/she participated, the comment had to build off another student's comment, connect to a historical event, or connect to present day. While students were free to speak as many times as they liked, there had to be at least three comments that did one of those three things. Because of the clarity, students understood the criteria, and there were no surprises; if a student only participated twice, he/she knew that only two of the three criteria were met, and would not receive full credit. While this rubric was not perfect by any means, (in fact, even Aaron was critical of it and passionate about reworking this rubric) it was a great place to start. Hopefully, through these examples, new teachers can see the level of detail needed when creating good rubrics.

The last large mistake in this category that I accidentally created involved the end-of-marking-period grading. It is simple to avoid this, yet difficult to execute. I got this advice from a local social studies supervisor at another district: never end a unit at the end of the marking period. Typically, a performance task or exam is required to show evidence of comprehension and retention at the end of the unit. However, if you use a calendar and plan the duration of every unit, you can ensure that marking periods end somewhere in the middle of any given unit. Therefore, students generally will have had their marking period grades weeks before the marking periods close. To illustrate, if a marking period ended on October 14, perhaps I would plan that my first unit would end on September 30 and my second unit would end on October 25. This is good planning because students would have had their heavily weighted assessments for the first unit two weeks before the marking period closed. Furthermore, there would, presumably, be no major grade-altering assessments in the beginning of the second unit. Therefore, students and parents would be aware of the grade well before the closing of the marking period. This will save students, and you, many headaches. Although it is incredibly hard to plan your first year before you have any experience, I would highly recommend laying basic unit foundations by organizing units around marking period end dates.

Conclusion

Minimize any surprises and problems through setting clear expectations, creating thorough rubrics, and managing unit durations. To set clear classroom procedures, make your expectations blunt and clear, and follow through with enforcing those expectations. To make rubrics, first make sure the assignment is rubric-worthy. Once you have determined that, make sure to be concrete and objective with your rubric's criteria. Lastly, to avoid parental and student complaints about marking period grades, organize your units such that the end of a unit never falls too close to the closing of a marking period (aside from the very last unit/marking period). These things will promote a positive class culture with clear expectations, explicit criteria for success, and curtail feelings of unfairness from students.

LESSON 13 – MAINTAIN YOUR CONFIDENCE.

Journal on August 20: "I am currently writing this in midst of a flurry of confusion, uncertain expectations, and a mind-numbing feeling of 'I have no idea what the hell I'm doing.' In a week's time, I will be attending teacher orientation for my school, where I hope to gather some information as to what I am expected to do during the year. Although I am typically collected and reserved, I do feel the nerves of the first day creeping..."

Journal on October 15: "...I printed all the materials for the class and looked through it – If I just keep acting like I know what I am doing, despite how untrue it is, I'll be fine..."

Journal on December 1: "...I question my choice of teaching as a career because of my ambivalent feelings, the lack of respect from those around me, the horrendous pay and financial benefits. I think Bo Burnham said it best that, 'If you can live your life without an audience, you should do *it.' Now, I have an audience every day who demand to be entertained constantly while my superiors demand more. A desk job would have been so much easier. The idealist in me loves my resilience and my decisions, yet the businessman in my mind is screaming for me to just get an MBA and work mindlessly until I die like everyone else. I think, despite my complaints, the idealist is still winning."*

Introduction

This was the first lesson I wrote down as a new teacher – a first-year teacher must always exude confidence, regardless if it exists. Within the first few days, I could see that other teachers, students, and administrators could sense my apprehensions. Your first year teaching is such a whirlwind of new, uncharted experiences that it is difficult to seem confident in a high-stress, daily-deadline-driven environment. Furthermore, when you have taken years of college level courses to prepare you for the first year, and yet you still seem lost, confidence is not the feeling that emerges. Nonetheless, you must muster up complete confidence in yourself, or at least be able to fake it. During the first section, I will focus on my short-lived delusion of preparedness out of college, my gaffes in class, and my career questioning. In the following section, I will write about my successes with confidence and ways to improve your confidence during your first year.

Failures

While a generally self-assured person, my first-year teaching revealed low confidence in numerous areas. The first element was the plummeting confidence throughout the transition from college and student teaching to my first-year teaching. Further, there were many times in class where I was understandably nervous, and I displayed that nervousness as opposed to faking confidence. Lastly, as mentioned in my semi-dramatic journal entry, I – for a period of my first-year teaching – became less confident in my overall decision to become a teacher.

Out of college, I felt ready for my first year teaching. Student teaching solidified this confidence, as there were numerous supports from cooperating teachers, university advisors, and professors. It is common for student teachers to feel confident in their abilities; the educational theories and models are fresh in your head from college, you have the support network needed, and you are ready to take on the world. However, after you land that first job, you realize that, without these supports, you feel lost. It was in early August before the school year when I truly started thinking about my upcoming first year; I had no clue what I was doing. Subtle surges of panic and anxiety surfaced when thinking about all the unknowns. Despite my experience student teaching, college courses, and long talks with former teachers and professors, I still felt unprepared and lacked confidence in myself.

Body language and tone are the phonetics of confidence, and I made mistakes with both in class;

students easily sensed my uncertainty. Not aware of it at the time, as my mind was focused on content instead of presentation, and I had a few nervous ticks. The first one was that I would scratch the back of my head when I felt unsure. I had no idea I was doing this until one day, I saw students sporadically laughing under their breath with one another. It occurred in intervals, and, while I did not call them out publicly, I was pondering the reasoning. Why were they laughing? Is a student misbehaving every few minutes, causing them to laugh? Was a student shining a laser pointer on me? It finally dawned on me that they were innocently laughing at my nervous tick. Every time I scratched the back of my head, students could not help but laugh as if to say, "Here he goes again." My body posture was also very casual. Despite being a decent public speaker in more formal settings, I would typically cross my legs, putting my weight on only one of my legs. I believe I did this during student teaching too, which is where I formed the habit, but there was a podium in that classroom to hide my posture: no such luck during my first-year teaching. Again, I had no awareness of this habit. Within the first few weeks, I asked Aaron – who was sometimes in my class while I was teaching – for some advice on improving my practice. I expected recommendations on the content, my activities, or student participation. Nope. He simply said, "You need to look confident, from your body positioning to how to say things." It was at this point that I realized I had given no thought as to how I was standing in class.

Throughout my first year teaching, my confidence in my career choice ebbed and flowed. This might catch criticism from lifelong teacher aspirers, who knew since they were young that they wanted to teach and would never think of leaving the profession. Nonetheless, I think it is common for the typical teacher to start questioning their choices. As displayed in my journal entry, there were many detriments to teaching: the pay is not great, the profession is publicly ridiculed, people (even family and friends) see your profession as a joke, it is emotionally draining, and you work long hours. This is not to say that every new teacher will face the doubt of his/her career, but it happened to me, so it is best to be prepared.

Successes

So, what are some strategies to combat these doubts and exude confidence? In regards to the confidence delusion you might feel after college and student teaching, you should, counterintuitively, underestimate your confidence. In my experience, it was the sharp and swift awakening that went from feeling confident and prepared to feeling helpless and lost that truly ruined my confidence; it was the shock factor that sent my mind spinning and made me so uncertain. Take this as an absolute: you will feel unconfident as a first-year teacher. There are no circumstances in which a new teacher feels prepared during those first few months. If I had been aware of this fact, I could have better sensed that my overconfidence after college and student teaching was an illusion, and the shock of going from confident to apprehensive was to be expected. This would have facilitated a smooth and realistic transition from pre-teaching to first-year teaching.

In class is perhaps the most important venue in which to exude confidence, despite if it truly exists. In Dave Burgess' well-known book, *Teach like a Pirate*, he argues that presentation is an overlooked element of lessons. While his book focuses more on showmanship and engaging activities, I think the takeaway is that an active and dynamic speaker, one that embodies confidence, will be seem more credible and more engaging than one who is not. Having nervous ticks, disheveled body language, and a shaky tone are all very common for new teachers; speaking in front of a crowd is difficult. However, it gets much easier with practice, preparation, and self-awareness. These three things are the remedy to feeling, or at least radiating, certainty in oneself. I would recommend getting as much practice as one can speaking in front of groups before the first year teaching. There are a few different ways one can achieve this. In my case, I got a small teaching job over the summer before my first year. I taught math, even though my certification was in social studies, to high schoolers twice a week through a local college program. This experience grew my confidence in my speaking ability. Despite my nervous head scratching tick and my not-so-perfect body language during my first year, my tone and voice control were excellent; I attribute this to my summer job experience. Another option that has gotten positive feedback is Toastmasters, an international organization that has localized chapters with the aim of growing public speaking skills, communication, and leadership. While I cannot speak to its effectiveness, I would suggest browsing the website if you feel you need to grow in this area. Another obvious solution to feeling unprepared and unconfident in class is to simply make sure you have your lesson thoroughly outlined. I will not write too much about this fact, as it is obvious, but having a detailed plan typically helps first-year teachers feel confident. I will note, however, that there will be *many* times where you will not thoroughly plan. In fact, there will be times where you hardly planned at all. One, nevertheless, needs to emit confidence in these situations. It can be difficult, but new teachers need to be aware of their nervous ticks; everyone has at least one. New teachers also need to be reflective with how they stand, walk, and speak in the classroom. It can be extremely difficult for people to pick up their own nervous tendencies. There are so many things to worry about in class that allocating a significant amount of attention to one's body positioning and tone can be unrealistic. If this is the case, I would recommend either asking another teacher in the class to track those elements, or videotaping yourself in class. These are easy and simple ways to monitor and improve your presentation skills and confidence in class. Remember, it is about *seeming* confident. Of course, it is best to actually feel confident, but the minimum goal here is to at least create the façade.

Lastly, in regards to the potential that one might feel unconfident in their career decision, I'm afraid I don't have much in the way of solutions other than time and the classic "fake it 'till you make it" rhetoric. Teaching is a peculiar profession in which one's confidence fluctuates regularly, sometimes even daily. If feeling demoralized, apathetic, or unconfident in one's career choice, simply give it some time. There will always be something that reinvigorates that passion and inspiration. Another strategy is act confident in your career choice – be happy that you took a stand to help others and that you are doing the best you can. While the principle is typically used as an in-class strategy, you can definitely use it as a personal strategy: act and you will become. Act happy, certain, and confident in your career choice, and you will become such. Obviously do not be disillusioned and maintain an unhappy profession just for the sake of it, but do be aware that this profession has extreme ups and downs. Hang in there – you will be happy you did.

Conclusion

A first-year teacher must maintain confidence, or at least convey confidence. You may feel confident after college or your student teaching experience; do not let that confidence overly materialize. It is better to go into your first year teaching with the expectation that you will feel a bit lost rather than go in overly confident and be shocked by the reality. Furthermore, you will have nervous ticks in class; perhaps a nervous scratch, a strange voice inflection, or untraditional body positioning. Fix these problems early through being self-aware, having another teacher in the room, or videotaping yourself. Lastly, you may feel a lack of confidence in your career choice at times. Try to give it some time – certainty will return.

LESSON 14 – MONITOR YOUR EMOTIONS.

Journal entry from October 22: "... *In regards to the past few months, it has been a quick series of ups and downs as a new teacher. A ton of stress followed by brief lulls, and then more stress and general apathy (it's the only way to be okay with my performance thus far). It has been crazy, although I am starting to get used to it. This first year teaching is a roller coaster; one day is great and I am convinced I want to do this forever, the next sucks and I want to quit. I'll continue, though."*

Introduction

The first year teaching is truly a roller coaster. As someone who does not often feel extreme emotions, I can say this past year has been one of the most emotionally trying years of my life. Many teachers, who typically have the "give" instinct before the "take", often struggle with carefully monitoring their emotions; they are more concerned with helping others before themselves. However, it is incredibly important to monitor emotions and react accordingly during your first year teaching. I will provide examples from my experiences of improperly and successfully monitoring my emotions, and the effect it had on my teaching and health.

Failures

Perhaps it depends on one's personality and fortitude, but I never took my accomplishments well. I never was happy, content, or satisfied; I simply achieved something and looked for the next goal. I had a high grade-point average, a major-specific valedictorian award, a job at one of the best secondary schools in the nation, and yet never felt pleased. This continued with my minute successes during my first year. While I ran a concert with students, I felt I could have done better. When I planned a unit, it could have had more student-driven activities. When I wrote an assessment, it could have been more authentic. I was not necessarily striving for perfection, but I simply thought the work I was doing was mediocre – and most of it was. However, I couldn't accept the fact that I had never done this before; this was my first-year teaching, and everything was new to me. It was not expected, nor feasible, for me to do everything well the first time. While I am specifically writing about teaching, this applies to most areas of life. Do you know how many revisions I have made to this book? And it is still flawed. However, one must find a delicate balance as a first-year teacher – one that applauds the attempt and constructively criticizes the result; one that congratulates the product but seeks improvements. I will discuss my recommendations of how to find this balance when discussing my successes in the "Successes" section.

I also occasionally took student comments personally. Luckily, I was in a school district where students were generally friendly and caring. However, there was one instance that occurred in the beginning months of my first year, in which the comment stung so much that I still feel some residual mental-aching. In my collaborative class with Aaron, I usually took a backseat – it wasn't good practice, but Aaron knew what he was doing, and I did not. My role was a special-education teacher in that class, but it would have ideally been to be a co-teacher along with Aaron – next year's goals. Anyway, a student in the class had an IEP, and he had some social awareness issues; he sometimes spoke before thinking of the consequences. One day in November, he had his hand raised, so I went over to help him. I forget exactly what the question was, but I helped the student, to which the student replied, "Thanks, whatever your name is." Now, note that the student absolutely knew my name; this was no honest mistake. This comment was a poke at the fact that I did not often engage in the class as a typical teacher. Rather, I helped individual students when they needed assistance and paid close attention to students with disabilities in the class. For some reason, I took that comment *very* personally. I did not get outwardly angry, but I did feel sadness, frustration, and anger in me. I remember having a slew of emotions:

"*I was doing the best I can; can't he see that?*" "*He's right, I suck at teaching.*" "*He should show me respect; I am

THE TEACHING MIRROR

his teacher." "Sure, I could be more active in class, but he shouldn't be saying that to me."

The thoughts continued racing in my head. He apologized later that day, which I appreciated, but my inability to let his comment go haunted me until my slight emotional breakdown that occurred the following month.

In early December, I had a partial emotional breakdown. It is very important to note that this was not a mental lapse of sorts; it was subtle, discreet, and unexpected. I do not want to paint the picture that I was having panic attacks and losing my mind; rather I was coming to grips that I could not deal with the emotional burden in the manner that I had been attempting to thus far. That day, I woke up feeling ill and experienced a wide range of emotions, from frustration to elation that I was not going into work. I had failed to successfully monitor my emotions for the first four months of my first year, and it took its toll. It was not until mid-afternoon that day that I realized that I was not sick at all; I simply buckled under the emotional stress of my first year. I took the first half of that day to reflect on my own happiness – I was not happy. For the first time in four months, I realized that I had not been checking in with my own emotions, and it was leading me to be personally unhappy, professionally unfulfilled, and emotionally drained. Upon this revelation, I drove myself to my undergraduate college, where I knew there was a mental health center, and sought therapeutic help.

Another teacher (whose name has been censored) had an eerily similar experience to me during their first-year teaching, which is why I think it is valuable to share. This teacher worked at a very different school, an urban school in a low-income area, during their first year teaching and, presumably, had much more strenuous conditions. Nonetheless, the stress you face during your first year is somewhat scalable; there is so much emotional pressure during your first year and teachers often feel a similar emotional burden, despite the conditions of the school district. This teacher explained to me, only half-jokingly, that they often thought about "driving into a concrete barrier on the commute home" during their first year. Perhaps my symptoms were not as severe, but I could absolutely empathize with this teacher's statements. Eventually, like me, this teacher had hit an emotional barrier, and sought therapy.

Successes

Emotions are a particular case where individuality and preference reign absolutely. I will discuss how I successfully monitored my emotions to cope with the first year, but above all else, one must find what works for him/her. I recommend carefully noting my experiences, adopting what you think might work, and finding a parallel path.

After my quasi-mental breakdown, I became much more concentrated on my emotions throughout the year. While I went to the mental health center for a therapist, I was turned away because I was no longer a student. A therapist would have been ideal, but I decided to try to cope with it myself. To do so, I started meditating a few minutes each day (although it more realistically became every few days) and journaled about my emotions. Again, this most likely isn't for everyone, but taking a few moments at the end or during the day to reflect on what happened cleared my mind effectively and allowed me to acknowledge the good and accept the bad. I had been journaling regularly about my teaching experience in preparation for this book, but I had focused more on the instructional and professional survival aspect rather than the emotional. I simply expanded these journals to include my thoughts and feelings on the occurrences of the day. After I journaled, I took ten or so minutes to meditate, and then resumed my nightly routine. Clearly, I am not suggesting every new teacher must journal or meditate, but having some outlet in which you can directly address the happenings throughout the day will be greatly beneficial. One of the most significant benefits is that meditating or journaling allows you to concretely establish your feelings, which makes the solution to those emotions strangely visible. It facilitated me in accepting my accomplishments, and provided that balance of pride and critique of my work. When you confine your emotions and feelings in your mind without an outlet, as I did for the first few months, your mind is foggy. Consequently, it is more difficult to define progressive steps towards actionable improvements. So, create an emotional venting system that works for you, one that allows you to address, not escape, the days' struggles.

 The anonymous teacher, whose experience I described previously, also sought therapy. During this teacher's first year teaching, it took longer than it took me to realize he needed an emotional vent. Nonetheless, it resulted in this teacher going to a therapist for over a year. I am not aware if he used other means to emotionally de-stress, and he did not tell the specifics of his therapy. Nevertheless, this teacher simply stated that it helped him, and that he would recommend it to others.

When I talk to other new or first-year teachers about this topic, they recoil. They say one of two things: either they know exactly where I am coming from, or they deny that their experience was at all similar. Whether it is the stigma of talking about therapy and emotional issues, especially for men, that causes the recoil, or whether speaking about it sparks a bad memory, I do not know. However, this shows to me two possibilities. The first is that most first-year teachers experience a similar emotional trauma and some teachers will not admit it for some reason. The second is that the level of emotional stress is completely subjective. Either way, it is valuable to be aware of your emotional state, and to nourish it if needed throughout the first year.

Conclusion

The first year is hard in a general sense, but it can be especially hard on your emotional state. Most first-year teachers that I know had some problems coping with the emotional demands of teaching, which caused a range of adverse effects. While personality, coping strategies, and stress management will determine one's emotional state throughout the first year, I recommend you set up an activity that allows you to emotionally vent. Perhaps journaling, meditation, or therapy might help; however, there are numerous additional options as well. The important thing is that you address the happenings of the day head-on; do not come home and binge into escapism on Netflix and the internet. Face the happenings of the day, both good and bad, and accept them through whatever coping system that works for you.

LESSON 15 – PRIORITIZE EVALUATIONS.

Journal on August 15: "…Much like I did in college, I plan on just playing the rubric. I printed out the lesson evaluation forms, which I found on the school's website. The strategy here is to simply make sure that I check off everything on those evaluations so that I can justify a high evaluation score…"

Journal on October 21: "This week has been alright. I feel bad, because I don't really know what I am doing, but I am trying to teach the best that I can. My US II class is going very well. I had my first observation this week and it went incredibly well. Typically, I have heard that (administrators) will try to give you a 2 in a category as a non-tenure, but I did very well and I believe I got a 3 or 4 in every area…"

Journal on November 29: "Just saw my first RateMyTeacher.com review – 5/5! The student says that I am the 'trillest teacher alive.' No idea what that means, but I'll take it. I have no idea which student it was, and I can't *even begin to guess, but it's nice to have some good feedback."*

Introduction

Evaluations: a source of sheer fright and worry for first-year teachers nationwide. Idealistically, evaluations should be a helpful tool to enhance your practice – but there is no denying it becomes a survival game, especially in your first year. There are a few evaluations that teachers are concerned with: lesson observations, summative evaluations, and student evaluations. Depending on your state, you will most likely have some combination of announced and unannounced lesson observations. I had two announced and one unannounced. I will discuss my somewhat poor performance on the unannounced observation and my disillusionment of student evaluations in the "failures" section. Then, I will address my reflective solutions, successes in the announced observations, perspective of student evaluations, and strategies for the summative evaluations. Note that my school district uses the Danielson Framework for evaluations, so any mentions of scoring are related to Danielson.

Failures

I did not fail on my unannounced observation, but I definitely did not do as well as I would have liked. I distinctly remember the quick burst of adrenaline that shot through my body when I saw an administrator sitting in my class when I walked in. I knew it had to come, but I was not feeling good about this lesson. Two lessons ago, we had a great class discussion. The lesson prior, we had a mini symposium where students presented modern-day amendment cases. However, the day of the observation, I was mainly lecturing, which does not do well during evaluations. That is how it goes, I'm afraid. I took a moment to calm myself before the bell rang to initiate the start of class, and then proceeded to the best of my ability. I tried to ask improvisational questions within the lecture – some hit, some missed. I also tried to make analogies with the content to relatable situations. Knowing that lecturing was exactly what an administrator did *not* want to see, I quickly got through it and moved on to an activity where students listened to and analyzed lyrics from the musical *Hamilton*. The lyrics paralleled the content, and I thought it was an engaging activity for students. I relaxed a bit at this stage of the lesson, as I thought the activity would surely win my administrator over. I closed the lesson smoothly and waited for the post-observation meeting with my principal.

My perception of the lesson and expectations were flipped upside-down at the meeting. My administrator stated that the lecture was comprehensive, but he took the majority of the time to criticize the activity. He was particularly harsh on the directions on the handout during the activity, something to which I had given little attention. He also gave more recommendations on closure for lessons, which I thought had gone smoothly. This was my third and final observation (I had my two announced observations already at this point), but I scored "Basic" in two areas.

While this information is unconfirmed, it was rumored that all first-year teachers would receive at least one "Basic" rating or below on their evaluations so that, if need be, administrators could use it as a reason to withhold the next year's contract. Essentially, it shielded the school from any potential lawsuits that could results in failing to rehire a first-year teacher. Whether this information is true or not, do not be too discouraged if you receive a somewhat low score on one of your evaluations – it is normal for first-year teachers.

Furthermore, I had become disillusioned with student evaluations. Many teachers passionately pursue "five stars" on RateMyTeacher.com, or similar student evaluation reports. Furthermore, while my district did not use them, some districts have formal student evaluations, which administrators take into consideration. When I got my first student feedback on RateMyTeacher.com, I was ecstatic that it was a five. It brewed a feeling of achievement and success – it did not matter what administrators thought. My students thought I was good, and that was enough. Well, that kind of thinking evaporated quickly. I will discuss the reasoning in the success section proceeding.

Successes

In regards to unannounced observations, they will never come at an opportune time. Despite my previous two lessons being stellar, the unannounced observation came on the day where I was doing a mediocre lesson that including a hefty amount of lecturing. It is unrealistic to have a phenomenal lesson every day in preparation for the unannounced observation. However, you can implement things that will make even your mediocre lessons structured well and impressive for administrators. Always have a do now, objective, and an agenda visible upon walk-in. Furthermore, make sure there is at least one student activity in each lesson. Lastly, make sure there is a closing that references the objective from the beginning. This is all standard, but if you embrace these elements into your daily lessons, you will never score poorly on an evaluation. You may receive a few scores that are lower than optimal, but you will be fine. You cannot plan for unannounced observations, but having a well-designed lesson structure will be impressive. In my case, I scored fairly well on my mediocre unannounced observation, largely because of my daily lesson structure. (A quick side note here: if your school uses Atlas Rubicon Mapper for their curriculum, and many do, you can be tipped off when an unannounced observation is happening. Under the "Activity" section, you can see when and who viewed your curriculum. If an administrator viewed your curriculum and your current unit, you can expect an observation soon. While this aside might be outdated in two years, when the next new curriculum mapper will inevitably replace Atlas, it is a valuable piece of information that I wished I had.)

There is a lot more freedom, mobility, and flexibility with announced observations. Usually, an announced observation is planned at least a week in advance, which gives you time to plan a progression of lessons that climax on your observation day. Furthermore, you can sometimes request which class and/or period you wish to be observed.

For my first observation, I planned a week's worth of lessons around simply acing the observation day. You should do the same. Regardless of the consequences on the planned unit, your evaluation scores are important, and the cost-benefit scale tips in favor of altering plans to make the observation lesson great. For my first observation, I planned a Harkness discussion, where students autonomously sat in a circle and discussed an article. In preparation for the observation, I had students do a practice Harkness two days prior, primed students with potential topics to discuss, and set the expectations. On the day of the observation, students moved their desks into a circle, started the discussion, and continued the discussion through the entire class period. The magic of this observation was that I – and this is no exaggeration – said six sentences the entire class. I welcomed students to class, asked them to get started, displayed a student contribution diagram, and then closed class. The rest was completely student-driven. To explain the aforementioned student contribution diagram, I was tracking student contributions on a seating chart that displayed the chronology of the conversation. Essentially, I drew a line to Student A to Student B to Student C when each spoke and built off each other's comments. At the midpoint of the class period, I projected an image of this student contribution chart to show which students spoke, and which students still needed to contribute. Through this lesson, I checked all the boxes: student-driven, incorporated technology, high-level questioning (I asked a closing question), and solid lesson structure. Because I planned ahead, even prepping my students for the ordeal, I received all "Proficient" or "Distinguished" scores.

Similarly, I prepped students for my second observation. While not as strong as my first, my second observation entailed students presenting arguments for and against America's strategy in the Philippines after the Spanish-American War from a military, political, and social standpoint. To prep students, I untruthfully told them that the administrator was going to be grading them on their presentation. Obviously, the administrator was grading me, but it made students concerned enough to prepare more for their presentation. While this might be ethically dubious, the main lesson still holds: your evaluations are extremely important. Nevertheless, in the same pattern as my last observation, I only said a few things in this lesson. I had an opening quote analysis activity, I provided some feedback after each presentation, and then I closed the lesson. I, again, received "Proficient" or "Distinguished" in all areas.

The big takeaways from my announced observations are simple, but all-important: prepare your students for the observation, make the observation lesson student-driven, and make the lessons well structured. In both announced observations, I did less. I only spoke when I needed to and let students do the rest. Administrators want to see students configuring the room layout, leading discussions, and taking initiative. While it would be ideal to have students doing this extremely often in your class, you should prepare your students to do this at least during the observations through practice runs and setting clear expectations.

I want to address one additional component of the formal observations: the post-observation meetings. After the announced or unannounced observations, teachers meet with the administrator who observed the class to discuss the lesson, conclusions, scores, and to suggest improvements. During this post-observation conversation, the administrator will ask you a series of questions, which varies by district. Nonetheless, the questions asked are often available on the teachers' section of the school district's website. In my case, I found the document on the website that listed out the questions administrators asked during post-observation meetings. I printed the sheet, hand wrote some bullet-pointed answers to each question, and brought it with me to the post-observation meetings. Not knowing the etiquette, I tried to keep my answer sheet hidden when in the meeting. I had one administrator comment about the sheet, saying that it was a smart idea, and one that other teachers rarely use. Make sure to check your district's website to see if the questions are available online.

While I used to be concerned with student evaluations and RateMyTeacher.com scores, I have learned that students are not good at evaluating teachers. Accordingly, student evaluations do not matter and are not good measures of performance. Do not confuse my assertions with saying students' opinions don't matter; students' feelings of you are very important. However, students do not have a good sense of what makes a good teacher. I learned this through two different avenues: demo lessons and investigating RateMyTeacher.com scores.

I had two demo lessons presented by job-seeking teachers in my class during my first year. The first demo lesson went poorly for the teacher; the lesson's objective was confusing, and the presentation made me empathetically cringe. At the end of the lesson, the administrators observing the demo lesson requested the potential new hire to leave the room, and asked students for their feedback: thumbs up, thumbs down, or thumbs to the side. Despite the glaring flaws in the demo lesson, almost every student put his/her thumb up. The administrator stated, "Wow, how very generous of you." Likewise, the second demo lesson went poorly – perhaps even worse than the first. Nonetheless, the majority of students put their thumbs up when asked for feedback. It could be that students just wanted to be nice, but it showed me that students are not good evaluators of teachers. Students judge a teacher by how funny he/she is and how difficult he/she is. Which leads me to RateMyTeacher.com.

On RateMyTeacher.com, I currently have purely five star reviews from students. I absolutely do not deserve five star reviews. Period. Reading through the comments, I could see why I have five stars. Reviews like, "such a good teacher, understandable and fun," or "...he's like a ray of sunshine," are evidence to me that I was rated highly because I was personable, humorous, and charming in class. These are a few attributes of a good teacher, but there are so many more important areas that RateMyTeacher.com does not assess. A good teacher would hold students to a high standard and enforce it: I did not. A good teacher would create a thoughtful and academic class culture: I did not. A good teacher would create meaningful and authentic lessons, performance tasks, and assessments: I did not. I may have been personable in class, but I was not a great teacher. RateMyTeacher.com is not a measure of a teacher's quality – please do not be too concerned with student reviews.

Lastly, teachers have summative evaluations. These evaluations occur at the end of the year, and a teacher must present evidence of parental contact, school community contributions/participation, and reflective practices. I had tremendous success in this area because I simply wrote down *everything* I did in a Google Document. Here is a sample of what it looked like:

> "10/14 - Participated in the school concert and interacted with students.
>
> 10/25 - Called Jack's and Diana's parents to compliment the hard work during the Harkness discussion.
>
> 11/3 - Played in the Faculty vs Students' Basketball game.
>
> 11/8 - Chaperoned the Girls' Basketball Practice from 3:30–5 p.m."

No matter how minute the action was, I recorded it. At the end of the year, I had over thirty pieces of solid evidence of parental communication and school community contributions. I would recommend you have a similar recording system for your activities. Record your participation as soon as you can – you will forget about it if you don't.

Conclusion

Succeeding in evaluative aspects of teaching during your first year is important, but it need not be overly stressful. For unannounced observations, prepare through always creating cohesive and well-structured lessons. You cannot possibly create tremendous lessons every day, but having every day lessons that are "good enough" will do. For announced observations, make sure you prepare students as much as you prepare yourself. Your evaluation scores depend on your students' interactions throughout the observed lesson; make sure students understand what you expect of them so that they, and you, will not fall flat on observation day. In regards to student evaluations and RateMyTeacher.com reviews, do not pay much attention to them. Typically, the easy and/or funny teachers rate highly, but that does not mean they are good teachers. Finally, for the summative evaluation, make sure to create a timely list of things you have done throughout the year. Prioritize your evaluations – know which matter, which do not, and prepare accordingly.

THE TEACHING MIRROR

"Good teaching is more

a giving of right questions

than a giving of right answers."

- Josef Albers

LESSON 16 – MAKE IT RELEVANT.

Journal on June 22: "...Because I was sitting next to him during graduation, I thought I would ask him for some advice. We got into a deep conversation about teaching, and the key points of being a good teacher. He said two things that remain in my mind: don't get complacent, and make it relevant..."

Introduction

How do you get students engaged as a first-year teacher? How do you get students excited and/or interested in pieces of content that you may even feel is boring? This is a common worry for first-year teachers, and one that I had throughout the year. The key to getting students engaged and interested in content is to make it relevant. I want to first address my failures throughout the year with making content authentic and relevant, and then outline my successes and advice for other first-year teachers.

Failures

There were many instances of failure in this area in my United States History I class. For most pieces of information presented, I found myself consistently asking, "So what? Who cares?" For instance, the United States History I curriculum called for teaching students very particular details about colonial America. Almost daily, I did not understand how the content would truly benefit students. Did they really need to know the differences in housing layouts between the Chesapeake Bay regions and the New England regions? Despite my confusion, I followed the typically dull curriculum, which involved lecturing, worksheets, and outline homework. While there were times in class where information would be relevant and contemporarily connected, most of the content presented in United States History I was taught in isolation. This was the greatest fault of the class: it rarely connected to present day. I grew frustrated at the curriculum and myself because I believed I was doing a disservice to students. I wanted to change the curriculum, or at least alter it to include more relevance, but I did not know how to do so.

One memory I have in particular, as explained in the journal entry, is asking a fellow teacher for advice during the last day of my first year. I asked him how to regularly make classes interesting and relevant for students. I asked, "For example, we finished a unit on the Mexican-American War recently. How could students really be interested in that? Sure, the war is important, but how could students really be engaged with that?" He inquired about what we did in class to study the war, and I told him that students looked at the differences between the accounts of American and Mexican generals during the war. He then replied that I could give a homework assignment in which students researched a modern conflict and provided two news articles from each side's perspective. Through doing this, I would solidify the importance of looking at perspectives, rather than simply the content. It was these ideas that I failed at creating throughout the year, and I had asked for advice on this topic too late to implement my discoveries.

The lack of relevance is a common mistake for both first-year teachers and veterans alike. History teachers may be particularly guilty of this, but there is no doubt that numerous subjects are void of authentic learning experiences that demonstrate the content's uses for students.

Successes

I also had some success with making content relevant. Most notably, the United States History II curriculum was created with relevancy in mind. We followed a "then and now" type of curriculum, where students would study historical time periods and then compare it to modern day. This was much more meaningful and successful than the United States I curriculum, and students enjoyed it more. Furthermore, the United States History I curriculum included *some* areas of relevancy. For example, students were able to connect slavery to modern-day mass incarceration and the Black Lives Matter movement.

THE TEACHING MIRROR

Nonetheless, most of these connections were weak and not fully established. Next year, this is one of the areas I want to work on most.

The biggest takeaway for readers is that every content area, no matter how boring, can be made relevant and interesting; my conversation with my colleague illustrated that point. Even the somewhat boring Mexican-American War can include a relevant and interesting modern-day assignment for students. There is nothing worse than students asking, "Why do we need to know this?" If students do not think it is important or interesting, they will be disengaged. There are a few ways that first-year teachers can make the content relevant, but it is usually content-specific. For social studies, I like to ask the question, "Why is x the way it is today?" Then, students could use history to understand the reasoning. For instance, I could show students present-day data on religion in America and ask, "Why are the overwhelming majority of Americans Christians today?" Then, students could study American immigration during the colonial America unit and see the connections. The teacher who discussed relevancy with me in my journal entry was a science teacher, and he gave me the example of asking students about their everyday observations. For instance, for a unit involving carbon dioxide, this teacher requested students to go home and weigh themselves at night, and then the following morning. The students noticed that they weighed less in the morning than at night. This teacher's question was, "Why do we weigh less in the morning? We did not just suddenly lose mass in our sleep, did we? So, what happened?" This sparked students' curiosity and engagement. Even you, the reader, want to know the answer now, don't you? That is why relevancy is so effective in class. This unveils the second key point: *everything* can be made relevant. It is your job to be a little creative and potentially take some risks, but we can achieve relevancy in even the dull content. If you can make it relevant, students will be engaged, and they will have a better learning experience because of it.

Conclusion

First-year teachers can ensure consistently meaningful and powerful lessons through making the content regularly relevant. While you do not have full control over what content needs to be taught, you can change how you teach the content. Ask yourself, "Why do students need to know this? Is there any way to make this piece of the content relate to students' lives or the current world?" I suggest you ground your relevancy in a single question in which students can explore through the content. If you can successfully make content relevant a few times a week, you will have an incredibly fulfilling and successful first year teaching.

THE TEACHING MIRROR

"Good teaching is

one-fourth preparation

and three-fourths theater."

- Gail Godwin

LESSON 17 – FIND A FITTING ORGANIZATIONAL METHOD.

Journal on September 11: "*So, that idea with having a computer folder for each student fell through. I tried it for like ten minutes, and then realized that it was dumb. I was sitting at the scanner just sending pages and pages through. I didn't have time for that....*"

Journal on October 15: "*...These manila folders are kind of trash, but they work...*"

Introduction

Organization is incredibly important as a teacher. One must keep track of class materials for numerous classes, past assignments, upcoming assignments, parental information, professional development hours, notes, and a constantly repopulating task list. While I struggled at first to find a good organizational method, I eventually found one that worked, although not tremendously well. I will first discuss my failed experiments at organization, along with the problem of adopting the organizational methods you have seen before. I will then address my successful organizational method, how I created it, its effectiveness, and room for improvement.

Failures

When I first tried to create an organizational system, I failed in three key ways. The first was that I tried to do too much. The second was that I had not accounted for mobility. The last was that I tried to use my cooperating teacher's organizational method, which was impractical.

When I first created my organizational system, I tried to make it extremely intricate. For class, I was going to use three-ring binders, with each section of the binder dedicated to different categories such as class handouts and homework. Furthermore, I was going to keep a computer folder for each student, and scan each student's work so that I could have virtual copies of everything. It became antithetical to the very meaning of organization. Organization is supposed to help you work more efficiently – I was organized to a point of inefficiency. I sustained this organizational method for less than a week, and then scrapped it.

The second mistake I made was that I did not account for mobility. I attempted to create organization in my classroom such as an in-out box for students, a location for students to get materials such as staples or tape, and I even considered having students take attendance autonomously through checking themselves in on a white board. I received these classroom procedures and organizational examples in

Find a Fitting Organizational Method

college. However, none of these were practical because I had to teach in three different classrooms. How could I have students sign in on a white board if I had to move classrooms in four minutes between the bells?

The last mistake I made was trying to use my cooperating teacher's organizational method from my student teaching experience. They say that organization is incredibly personalized, and that using others' methods simply does not work well. This has some truth to it. However, I think the biggest problem was that the organizational method that my cooperating teacher used worked well for a teacher who was absolutely prepared, and has done the same or similar things in class for years. My organization *had* to be fundamentally different, because I was in a completely different situation. My cooperating teacher had binders chronologically filled with lesson plans and their corresponding handouts, PowerPoints, and homework. I was starting from scratch. All of these failures factored into finding a makeshift organizational system that worked for me.

Successes

To preface, my organizational system is very far from the best. In fact, I do not recommend you adopt much of this into your own practice. However, it is valuable to see how one forms one's own organizational method out of necessity and practicality.

My organizational method for classes consisted of ten manila folders, two for each class. One manila folder per class was dedicated for immediate lesson materials. I brought the corresponding manila folder to each class, and the folder consisted of a lesson plan, any physical materials needed, and usually some scribbled notes reminding me to make an announcement or to check in with a student. The other manila folder for each class was a work-to-do folder, where I would keep students' essays that needed to be graded, planning material for a lesson in the near future, and other miscellaneous materials for the class. The manila folder method had drawbacks: manila folders have no pockets, they are not durable, and things can fall out easily. However, I had a lot of success using this method for classes. The biggest advantage was that I only needed to take two manila folders to class with me, which made it very portable for my mobile schedule.

While I discarded my idea of scanning all student work, I suggest making use of online storage tools. I used Google Drive for quick and portable storage, and it allowed me to organize materials by class and by unit. Other alternatives are Dropbox and OneDrive. Use whatever you feel comfortable with, but do not have physical copies of everything that you do for the year. If you need It before a class, print it out and then recycle the leftovers. Papers start piling up quick as it is, and keeping physical copies of everything that you are doing is just cumbersome.

To keep up-to-date on tasks that needed to be completed, I simply wrote a to-do list on a post-it note and stuck it to my computer. This list was reserved for mundane things that I needed to do promptly. I also have a horrendous memory, so I absolutely needed this. Examples included things such as "Email AJ" or "Print copies for tomorrow." Once I had completed everything on the post-it note, I would trash it, and start another one. This helped me stay on top of the little things.

It is clear that my organizational method is very simple, and somewhat effective. The important thing is that it worked for me, given the limitations and restrictions I was faced with. It allowed me to be mobile, it was flexible for a new teacher's sometimes scattered planning, and it made sense to me. You should use a fitting organizational system that works for your given situation. There is no "best" organizational system for every teacher, as teachers have unique preferences, with unique schedules, and unique needs.

Conclusion

It is extremely difficult to develop an organizational plan before you start your first year, as it is difficult to anticipate the small details of your schedule, room locations, and level of flexibility needed. Nonetheless, you should develop an organizational style that fits your particular needs during the year. If you are only teaching in one room, perhaps consider a more rooted organizational system. However, if you need to be mobile, commit to a less cumbersome organizational system – less is often more in these cases. Lastly, do not attempt to use others' organizational models in their entirety, as it will not be useful in your particular situation.

LESSON 18 – FIND A FITTING CLASSROOM MANAGEMENT STYLE.

Journal on August 20: "… Luckily, I was shown my room for the first time a few weeks ago; it was void of furniture or decorations. I am not a very artsy person, and I also am told I am sharing the room with another teacher. How does that work? Do I decorate portions of the classroom, and he decorates other parts? Does the teacher with the most time in the class decorate the classroom? Do we decorate at all? Is this school 'too good' for decorations?"

Journal on September 2: "…I felt stupid not bringing anything (decorations). Aaron brought a globe, typewriter, posters, and a vintage American flag to hang up. I brought some folders…"

Introduction

Classroom management is more than student discipline and expectations; it extends to a spectrum of topics like decorations and classroom layout. While some of these topics are covered in college courses, many nuances are overlooked or not addressed at all. I will first discuss my failures regarding decorating my room, my class layouts, and disciplining students. I will then address the successes with my class layout and with discipline issues.

Failures

I abysmally failed at decorating my room. There seems to be two schools of thought with new teachers in this area: one cannot wait to decorate their room; the other has given no thought to it. I was in the latter group. I had only seen my room once a few days prior to the start of school, and I had no idea where teachers bought those inspirational posters. I decided to forgo the whole ordeal of decorating. Luckily, I had Aaron with me, and he had plenty of decorations to take up the entire room. If I had a bare room to myself, it would have looked atrocious. Whether you have a roommate or not, get some content-related decorations for your room before the school year starts. You do not need many to start, as you will find yourself randomly accumulating posters and decorations from other teachers and even textbook companies. Furthermore, you will want to leave some space for student work.

Find a Fitting Classroom Management Style

Nonetheless, learn from my mistakes and buy *something* decorative.

I also failed in regards to classroom layout for one of my classes. As a reminder, I taught in three different classrooms during my first year, which meant I had three chances to try classroom layouts. I reserved one of my United States History I classes to be my experimental group. I tried three different layouts with this class. The first layout consisted of the typical school rows. This worked well for when I was lecturing, but I did not like the feel of the classroom – students were not encouraged to interact. After about two months, I radically altered the room into one giant circle. Students could interact freely, and I was not the center of attention at the front of the room. However, this layout took up way too much room space, made it difficult to navigate through the sea of desks, and encouraged off-task behavior. Lastly, I tried to have students in groups of four or five. This layout worked fairly well, but it again encouraged students to talk while I was talking. I also did not like how I could not see some of the students' faces, as some were turned away from me. Each layout lasted a few weeks, but none of these classroom layouts fit my style well.

Lastly, I failed with classroom management by trying to overcompensate for my leniency through being too publicly strict to students in a few cases. There was one class in particular where Aaron would always be at his desk while I was teaching. Trying to show my management abilities, I would often be unnaturally strict to these students. There was one case where a student was talking while I was giving directions. I said something like, "[student's name], when I'm speaking, you need to be listening. Especially when I am giving directions, you need to be paying attention. I will not repeat myself. Understand?" I suppose it was also the tone in which I said it, as I realize now after writing my response that my retort doesn't give the impression of being harshly strict. After class, Aaron mentioned my behavior towards the student. He stated that the harsh backlash did not fit the undesired behavior. Ironically, in trying to have Aaron perceive me as a teacher who could control the classroom, I actually had gone too far with my control. There was another time in the same class where I asked for attention, and students did not give it to me within the few seconds I gave them. I asked for attention again, raising my voice. I had not realized how loud I got, but one of the students said, "Guys, quiet down; he is getting mad." I replied with a head nod. Looking back at the situation now, it was a mistake on two fronts. The first is that I raised my voice. A teacher should never have to raise his/her voice at their class – it is immature and loses respect. Furthermore, I should not have nodded my head, affirming that I was getting angry. If I remember correctly, I did not feel anger. I simply thought by saying I was angry, students would be controlled quicker. It is never a good idea to lead students to believe they can control your emotions. The common problem for new teachers is that they have emotions in which they cannot contain. My problem was that I did not have any emotions, but presented as if I did. Both net the same outcome: a loss of respect.

Find a Fitting Classroom Management Style

Successes

I did find eventual success in my classroom layout. While the experimental class never optimized, one of my other classes fit my teaching philosophy well. I like to feel in control of the classroom, but I also enjoy student discussions, collaboration, and group work. Accordingly, my U-shaped classroom layout allowed me to be in the front of the room, students to work in pairs, and whole class discussions. Lastly, by rotating one side of the "L" shapes, it was very easy to create groups for small group work or a larger debate group. I will diagram these explanations below. While usable with individual desks, note that my school uses tables instead (as shown in Figure 2 and Figure 3).

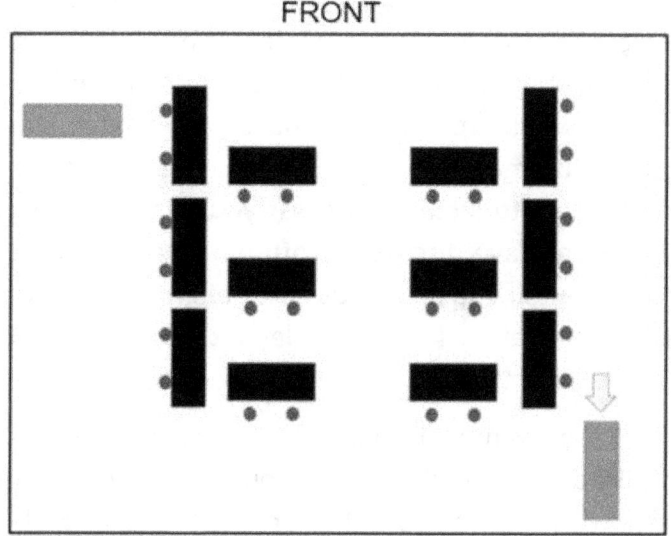

Figure 2: Typical Classroom Setup

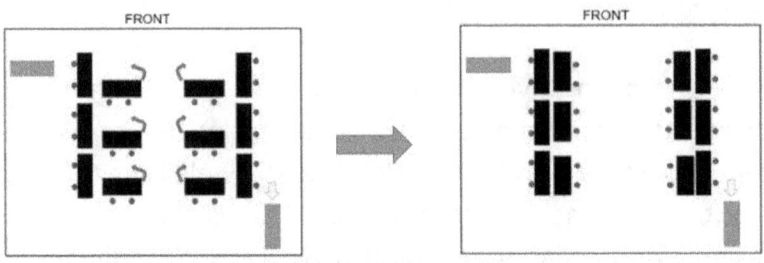

Figure 3: Transition to group work or large-table debate work.

As you can see from Figure 3, this allows for either six groups of four students, or two large groups of twelve students.

However, there were logistical drawbacks to this classroom layout. Most annoyingly, my desk was in the back of the room (the desk with the arrow over it Figure 2 and Figure 3). Since I did not have a presentation clicker, I would have to walk from the front of the room to the back to change slides when giving a presentation. Overall, though, I feel that this layout was the most versatile and dynamic. While I would recommend having a similar classroom layout, it ultimately depends on your teaching style. If you are planning to lecture for most your classes, use rows. If you plan to have discussions often, use groups or a whole circle layout. If you plan to use a lot of group work, then use groups. However, I think my layout has the flexibility to become all of those quickly, if need be.

Through my mishandling of student discipline issues, I realized that publicly calling out students for behavior rarely works. Doing so either breaks the relationship with the student, embarrasses him/her in front of classmates, or creates a power struggle where the student retaliates.

Instead, I started solving all behavioral issues by discussing the matter with the student in a one-on-one environment. You can do this in class too, so long as the attention of other students is elsewhere. There were two examples of student misbehaviors that I was able to solve easily and privately. The first was when a student, before the bell rang, yelled, "Why don't you shut the hell up!" at another student in class, and then proceeded to cry. Instead of making a scene, I asked students to work on the do-now assignment and made my way to the crying student. I asked him what was wrong, and he explained that he had received a poor score on an assignment in the previous class, and another student made a rude comment about it to him. He apologized, went to the water fountain for a drink, and was fine for the rest of the class. Had I engaged him in a public setting, without the knowledge that he was angry due to a grade, I could have made matters much worse. Similarly, I had a more chronic problem with another student in a different class who had the tendency to rudely put down other students in the class. This happened about eight times during the school year, and each time I settled the matter privately with the students involved. While I recommend that you settle all matters of behavior privately, I do realize that some teachers have a higher effectiveness through settling matters publicly, especially if the undesirable behavior occurs publicly. If the whole class heard it, many teachers will address the whole class as opposed to privately. While there is value to that statement, I have found it best as a first-year teacher to settle matters privately. Nonetheless, new teachers should discipline students in a manner that fits how they teach.

Conclusion

There are many different ways to manage a classroom in regards to layout, presentation, and student discipline. While new teachers discuss these strategies in teacher-education classes, the important part is sometimes absent: find what fits your style. Decorate your classroom with content-related artifacts and posters. In regards to classroom layout, I think my layout is dynamic and very transferable. As such, I would recommend adopting parts of the layout. Handling student discipline issues may be even more personalized. I recommend not confronting large behavioral issues in a public setting unless you already spoke to the student(s) privately. However, you may do so if you have a more authoritarian style (and there is nothing wrong with that!).

LESSON 19 – EXPERIMENT.

Journal on March 4: "...I tried that Harkness thing again today. I really like them, but something is still not right. Like, students enjoy them for the most part, and I do too, but there is something missing. I think I'll try doing one in my other class that puts them in smaller groups. I don't know. I'll see what happens..."

Introduction

While participating at a new teachers' panel at my undergraduate college, an aspiring teacher asked me, "What is one piece of advice you would give to new teachers or student teachers?" I responded with, "Fail often. If you are not failing, you are not experimenting. And, if you are not experimenting, you are not improving." Experimenting is essential to succeed. A first-year teacher needs to determine the styles and methods that work for him/her, and there is no better way than experimenting. I failed during my first year with some experiments and my frequency of trying them. Furthermore, I succeeded through these failures, but also conducted a few experiments that went well.

Failures

In my United States History I class, a group of teachers and I experimented with the creation of a musical project. The class topic at the time was Jefferson's presidency, and so – given that the musical Hamilton was popular at the time – we decided to create a project called "Jefferson the Musical." In this project, I assigned students a topic of Jefferson's life such as his childhood, early political career, presidency, etc. Then, students needed to create lyrics, record the song, and produce a music video that infused historical facts from their assigned topic. It sounded like an imaginative project that could engage students and execute smoothly. It did not. Other teachers, who had heard about the project from student complaints, began to warn us of the repercussions of the assigned project: parents will complain that the project is about musical talent, the project was too much for students, and that there had to be other non-musical options available to students. While I adjusted the project, I assigned it more or less how I originally conceived it to be. What a headache that project was. It solicited an enormous amount of complaints and logistical problems for weeks. I consider this experimental project a failure, but it taught numerous lessons about things to consider when designing creative projects.

Another failure of mine was my refusal to experiment. Understandably, as a first-year teacher, I wanted my classes to run as smooth as possible. As such, I was apprehensive at times with trying new things in class. One of my biggest regrets is my failure to spearhead a critical thinking curriculum for a project. I had worked for weeks with the Army's University of Military and Cultural Studies and created a usable curriculum with them. I got approval from my administrators to pilot the project, but I did not because I was afraid of trying something so abstract and novel. These apprehensions restrained me throughout the year, and I reflect with feelings of squander and contrite.

Successes

Although I classify my previously listed memories as failures, there are imbedded successes – that is the nature of experimenting. I understood what *didn't* work, which has and will guide my practice moving forward. From the "Jefferson the Musical" project, I learned that creative projects are possible, but the teacher must give students options. Perhaps giving students the option of a musical, poem, or research paper would have sufficed. Options are important with creative projects because it allows students who do not feel comfortable with the creative component an alternative. I also learned that setting realistic deadlines, and even sometimes working those deadlines out with students, is a necessity. A common problem for new teachers is the lack of awareness in regards to the assigned workload; we expect students to do too much in too little time. In the future, I may assign creative projects, but I will ensure these revisions are established.

As mentioned previously, I experimented with my personality in the classroom, my classroom layout, technology use, and my organizational system. In fact, most of this book is simply discussing the results of my yearlong experiments. However, I also experimented within the class as well, which went very well. For example, I once allowed students in my United States History II class to create their own project. We had a class discussion for a chunk of the class period about what they wanted to do, how they wanted to present it, and how it was to be graded. After some predictable "How about we just get an A" comments, students actually started creating a fair and worthwhile project that involved group debates. The result was spectacularly successful. Students were invested in the project as they had heavily influenced its creation, and they submitted high quality work. While I would not recommend this for every class, and certainly not every project, the larger idea is that I had no idea what would come of appointing students as project creators. I experimented, and it went well; that should be the takeaway.

One of my biggest successes was my use of Harkness discussions. I had been fascinated with Harkness discussions after viewing some colleagues conduct them, and I also researched Phillips Exeter Academy's use of these discussions. I experimented with Harkness discussions in every class, and tried conducting them in different ways. During one discussion, I created the questions and guided the class conversation; in another discussion, I allowed students to create the questions and guide the dialog; in yet another attempt, I broke the class into four smaller groups and had students discuss in the smaller format. I likely tried five or six different formats for the Harkness, noting which elements were successful and which needed altering. My findings were that there were a few valuable formats, depending on the discussion desired. For a whole class discussion, it was best to assign two students as "discussion leaders," who would generate three discussion questions and post them to Edmodo or Google Classroom the night prior to the discussion. For smaller group discussions, having one group leader in each small group worked well. Again, while this particular example and the corresponding findings might be valuable to some new teachers, the larger picture is to experiment – do not feel apprehensive or afraid. You will make mistakes and your experiments will fail, but first-year teachers develop through conflict, improve from failures, and grow from those experiences.

Conclusion

It is natural to feel uncomfortable with experimenting in class; however, it is a necessary and crucial element of the first year teaching experience. Try different things in class, and take note of the results. This is, of course, too easy – the hardest part is not the experimenting itself; it is overcoming the apprehensions of trying those different strategies. Defeat those feelings, as it will make you a better teacher. Even more beneficial, (most) administrators enjoy first-year teachers' attempts at new things. If you are feeling very unsure about an experiment, ask a supervisor or trusted colleague for their opinion of it. Nonetheless, make sure to experiment throughout your first year, and beyond.

LESSON 20 – BE REFLECTIVE.

Journal on June 15: "...Despite the pain in the ass that it was, I am glad I kept this journal. Well, at least I tried – it was supposed to be once a day I think, but once a week or so isn't bad..."

Journal on June 22: "Thank god this first year is over. I went to graduation, and I will miss many of those kids. But I am still glad I survived this year. I want to take a week to relax, and then I want to start redoing everything again..."

Introduction

The entirety of this book has been a grand reflective experiment for me, and the clarity it has brought to my first year has been palpable and helpful. Though being one of the core tenets of teaching, being properly reflective can be extremely difficult throughout the first-year teaching. I will first discuss my failures in my reflective practices, along with some reasons for those failures. Then, I will elaborate on my successes and the importance of being continually reflective.

Failures

Although I kept journals throughout my first-year teaching, I did not use them to inform my teaching enough. While the journals were, at least in some part, written to supplement this book, they were a good practice. I would recommend keeping a journal of sorts during your first-year teaching. However, the use of these journal entries was limited in my case. Perhaps because the end goal of the journal entries was for this book and not to guide my instruction. If I had used my journal entries, or written them in a different and more instructionally reflective-friendly manner, I would have been a much better teacher during my first year.

Another mistake I made was being indifferent about taking notes on individual lessons. Now, with my second year approaching, I have no useful memory of the effectiveness of particular lessons. Thus, despite already having done the lessons once, I must guess as to their potential effectiveness. Furthermore, for the lessons in which I did note its effectiveness, I threw away all of my past materials. Even if those notes remained, they are in a pile of other past papers and generally unfindable. I would recommend having an organized system to be reflective. Perhaps a daily Google Doc where you log the lesson and quickly make a few notes about it. This will help prepare you for your second year.

Lastly, and somewhat ironically, I think I took too many peoples' advice. Before my first year, I asked my former teachers, professors, and friends for potential tricks to cope with the upcoming year. Though there were many jewels in their advice, there were also many duds. Some pieces of advice were actually harmful to my professional growth. The great advice is easily recognizable as such, and the trash advice usually seems as such too. Despite that fact, first-year teachers, self-admittedly having no idea of the realities of the first year teaching, accept both good and bad pieces of advice as truths. As such, I suggest you take only some of the advice from others – including from this book.

Successes

I think my most obvious and concrete example of my success in this area is this book. While it may not be spectacular, writing it has been mutually beneficial (I hope). While I do not suggest you write a book on your experiences – I don't need the competition – I would suggest reserving time after your first year to process and reflect on the entirety of the year, and your lessons learned. Furthermore, as alluded to previously, I would suggest keeping a journal of both your instruction and emotions. If possible, review your journal each week to improve your practice and bring conscious your emotional state; this will make you a better teacher and avoid burnout.

Above all, plan to survive your first-year teaching, be reflective, and make your second year great. The first year teaching will always be hard, no matter how much you prepare, no matter how much you read, no matter how many people you ask for advice. You can only do so much during your first year, and trying to do too much could result in burnout, physically, mentally, and emotionally. Instead, go into the first year knowing that you will make mistakes, struggle, fail, feel angry and frustrated, perceive yourself to be a mediocre or bad teacher, and work more than you ever have. However, if you use some common sense – and some of the lessons from this book – you will be able to manage all of these obstacles, overcome them, and find success. Use these experiences during your first year to prepare to have a *great* second year teaching.

Conclusion

Being reflective is hard – *really* hard. While I succeeded in being reflective in some manners, I think there was a lot of room for improvement. I would suggest to first-year teachers to keep a journal that outlines your emotions, thoughts, and experiences both in and out of the classroom. Writing breeds clarity, which is a needed commodity during your first year teaching.

Furthermore, I suggest first-year teachers arrange an organizational method that allows you to track the effectiveness, timing, and other significant notes of daily lesson plans. Though I have not tried doing so yet (I will this upcoming year), I plan to use a Google Doc each day that lists the lesson and a few notes. Moreover, new teachers should not accept all advice blindly; just because someone has been in education his/her whole life does not mean they have a reservoir of great advice. Lastly, first-year teachers should plan to simply survive the first year, and each subsequent year feel progressively more confident, organized, and effective.

THE TEACHING MIRROR

"Effective teaching may be the hardest job there is."

- William Glasser

FINAL THOUGHTS

When you chose the field of education as your profession, you chose to embark on a journey – a journey filled with failure and triumph, agony and euphoria, frustration and forgiveness. During that first year, your mind will constantly be pedaling ideas, the workload will be exponentially growing, the stress will feel overbearing, the daily grind will be exhausting – and then, in June, it just *stops*. After ten months of resilience and perseverance, you will look back with nostalgia.

All of the included lessons in this book will help you prepare for the first year, but one overarching theme supersedes all of the included lessons: enjoy your first-year teaching. You will never again experience the unique blend of emotions that emerge during the first year. Not only will you learn extremely valuable things to improve professionally, you will also learn incredible things about yourself. You will not be the same person you were when you first stepped through your classroom door, and this is an exclusive aspect of the teaching profession.

When you have finished your first year, *you* will have been the one who took the plunge into the unknown. *You* will have helped students grow personally and academically. *You* will have worked long hours to create engaging classes. *You* will have sacrificed your time and energy for your students. *You* will have overcome seemingly impossible obstacles. Moreover, *you* will have made a difference. Be proud of all these things.

When I think of you, the reader, I see a reflection of me. I see a teacher with those nervous jitters and excited butterflies before that first day. I see a teacher who feels lost and unsure during those first few weeks. I see a teacher with endless potential, and I see a teacher with so many fantastic things to experience throughout that first year.

Teaching is a journey. Now it is time for yours.

ABOUT THE AUTHOR

Victor Z. Stanhope is now a third-year social studies teacher at his current school district. He is now a leader teacher at his district, working with administration to develop school goals, leading teacher-research teams, and still striving to give his students nothing short of his best. Victor will continue his work to enhance his teaching, and is currently working with local universities to provide professional development for teachers to improve in-class discussions. In his spare time, Victor enjoys reading great books, listening to and making music, and spending quality time with loved ones.

For legal and protective reasons, this book was published under a pseudonym.

www.ingramcontent.com/pod-product-compliance
Lightning Source LLC
LaVergne TN
LVHW051834080426
835512LV00018B/2870